PUSHCHAIR PATHS
East Midlands

Melanie Ramet

Published by Sigma Leisure – an imprint of
Sigma Press, 5 Alton Road, Wilmslow, Cheshire SK9 5DY, England.

British Library Cataloguing in Publication Data
A CIP record for this book is available from the British Library.

ISBN: 1 85058 826 0

Typesetting and Design by: Sigma Press, Wilmslow, Cheshire.

Cover photograph: Mel and Toby enjoying Bradgate Park
(Emma Adams)

Photographs: Taken by Melanie Ramet; pictures of the author taken by Antony Graham or Emma Adams

Maps: Bute Cartographics. Reproduced from Ordnance Survey mapping on behalf of The Controller of Her Majesty's Stationery Office. © Crown Copyright. Licence Number MC 100032058

Printed by: Bell & Bain Ltd, Glasgow

Disclaimer: the information in this book is given in good faith and is believed to be correct at the time of publication. No responsibility is accepted by either the author or publisher for errors or omissions, or for any loss or injury howsoever caused. Only you can judge your own fitness, competence and experience. Do not rely solely on sketch maps for navigation; we strongly recommend the use of appropriate Ordnance Survey (or equivalent) maps.

Foreword for new mums

Judith Lee: Clinical Specialist
Women's Health Physiotherapist

ORPing (Off Road Pushchairing) your way to health and fitness after having your baby – what a simple and fun way to do it!

I hope pregnancy and childbirth has been a wonderful and rewarding experience for you, but ladies, what has it done to your bodies? Despite your diligence with those tummy and pelvic floor exercises, are there parts of you that just don't seem quite the same?

What better way to tone tums and bums, than a good brisk walk? It will improve your posture, take inches off your waist, improve your stamina and circulation, and yes, it will do wonders for your pelvic floor.

If you have just had your baby, I suggest you start with very gentle local walks during the first 6 weeks after childbirth. Then gradually build up your speed and distance that you walk. Remember that all exercise should be pain free, so seek help from your GP, or Obstetric Physiotherapist if you have ongoing back or pelvic pain. You will be more comfortable if you wear supportive shoes, and, if breastfeeding, a really good-fitting bra.

You will want to give your children the very best, so indulge them in fresh air, and an early sense of adventure, but most of all, give them the Mum they deserve, one that is fit, strong and full of energy. ORPing will help you to achieve that.

Health promotion is high on the agenda of all health professionals, and I have no hesitation in recommending this book as an excellent example of a simple and fun way to set you on the road to better health.

Melanie has literally done the groundwork for you – simply follow in her footsteps and enjoy!

Judith Lee

Preface

We used to walk the Lakeland Fells and the mountains of Scotland. We used to hurl ourselves down hillsides on two wheels. Life was work in the week, dreaming of the hills. Weekends were out anywhere and everywhere by foot or by wheel.

Then baby Toby arrived and our world turned upside down. Our need to reach to the outdoors for sanity was now even greater. However, our first trips opened our eyes to irritating pushchair obstacles that we had previously taken in our stride.

The countryside had suddenly become more challenging; now it wasn't a matter of "where shall we go?" it was more "can we do this with a pushchair?" We needed a book that would tell us where we could go for a breath of fresh air, that wasn't too far, where the paths were fit for three plus wheels, that was safe if I went alone, and where the whole family could have a good time. Most of all we wanted routes that were easy to follow, as we were too tired to bother reading rambling route text. As new parents we couldn't find any such guidebook. So, we decided to write one.

We have scoured the East Midlands for the best simple and safe locations to take wheels out for a walk without obstacles. It's been great fun exploring the many shires of the East Midlands, visiting the summits and the lakes, the extensive forests and the great Halls.

In doing so, we coined the phrase "ORPing". This stands for "Off Road Pushchairing". We decided that all ORPing routes would transfer ORPers (pram pushers) from fume-laden pavements to the safety and peace of the countryside. They may also incorporate the possibility of a scrumptious home-made cake – why not, if you've made it out with a kiddy, you deserve it!

We have prepared 30 ORPing routes that include a route description, and a simple map to follow. This way, all you have to do is decide where you want to go, have a quick read, and follow the route – even if you're keen and go twice a month, this book will last you well over a year! These routes were researched over the winter months, and were still thoroughly enjoyable, so we know they are all weather walks.

As it's not good for the ego to turn back, the majority of our routes are circular and all tracks are TTT'd (Toby Tried and Tested).

ORPing routes vary from short walk on flat terrain, to an epic push on demanding tracks. The routes are graded depending on the distance, terrain and facilities available. We didn't spend much money on our days out, so they are a cheap option too.

Go on, grab the Granny or enjoy a day out with the baby group – it doesn't matter, just get ORPing. Enjoy this guide and we hope you find it as useful as a good night's sleep.

Happy ORPing!

Acknowledgements

Thanks are due in the most part to Toby, who has endured months of his mother chugging him round the countryside in search of wonderful pushchair paths. Secondly, Antony deserves a huge thank you for keeping a smile on his face as he sat at work and his family happily texted him from coffee shops and hilltops. Thank you also to Judith Lee, Sam Wakefield, Emma Adams and Sylvie Ancey for their enthusiasm and support. To Dad, Gina, David, Clare and Jane whose assistance with Toby, and constant interest in this guide are much appreciated. Our friends deserve a mention too, because we haven't seen them for months. Finally, much appreciation is given to the many individuals we met along the routes – their local knowledge has helped us find the best pushchair paths around.

Dedication

For Toby, our little explorer

Contents

About this Guide

Walk Categories   1
Walk descriptions   2
Toddle-tastic Sites   3
Equipment   3
Safety en route   6
Respect the Countryside   6
The National Forest   7
ORPing routes at a glance   8
ORPing: a positive experience ... 10

Ambles!

1. Belton House   12
Distance: Circular 2km
Terrain: Gravel and woodland paths, one lakeshore bridge may be too narrow for double buggies.

2. Bradgate Ruins   16
Distance: There and back 5.5km
Terrain: Surfaced flat path

3. Branston Water   19
Distance: Circular, 2km
Terrain: Flat, broad, loose stone track

4. Burrough Hill   22
Distance: There and back, 1.1km
Terrain: Loose stone and grass track.

5. Cresswell Crags   24
Distance: Circular, 1.2km
Terrain: Flat compact path

6. Highfields Loop   27
Distance: Circular, 2km
Terrain: Part tarmac, part gravel track, flat with one minor ascent

7. Mill Lakes 30
Distance: Circular, 3.5km
Terrain: Compacted gravel paths with some
woodland tracks.

8. National Memorial Arboretum 33
Distance: Circular, 2km
Terrain: Flat, broad surfaced or grass trails

9. Poulter Summit 36
Distance: Circular, 2km
Terrain: Gravel and grass tracks, one ascent

10. Rosliston 39
Distance: Circular, 3km
Terrain: Generally flat, broad, loose stone track

11. Rufford Abbey 42
Distance: Circular, 2km
Terrain: Broad surfaced or gravel track

12. Rushcliffe Country Park 45
Distance: Circular, 3km
Terrain: Broad, smooth gravel track, flat with one
minor ascent

13. Sherwood Forest 48
Distance: Circular, 2km
Terrain: Flat broad paths, circular

Rambles!

14. Attenborough Nature Reserve 52
Distance: Circular, 5.3km
Terrain: Flat compact paths, potential to be muddy in
wet weather

15. Beacon Hill 55
Distance: Circular, 4km
Terrain: Loose stone track, with one ascent to
Beacon Hill

16. Bestwood Colliery 58
Distance: Circular, 2.5km
Terrain: Compact paths with some grass tracks.
Steep ascent to the summit.

17. Big Wood 61
Distance: Circular, 4km
Terrain: Compact woodland paths and surfaced road

18. Clumber Lake 64
Distance: Circular, 5km
Terrain: Woodland tracks

19. Hambleton Peninsula 67
Distance: Circular, 7km
Terrain: Loose stone track, broad and undulating

20. Kedleston Hall 70
Distance: Circular, 5.3km
Terrain: Compact gravel paths with some woodland and grass tracks.

21. Sence Valley 73
Distance: Circular, 2.3km
Terrain: Flat, broad, loose stone track.

22. Shipley Circuit 77
Distance: Circular, 5km
Terrain: Surfaced paths and bridleways, some woodland paths

23. Thornton Reservoir 81
Distance: Circular, 5km
Terrain: Flat, broad, loose stone track

24. Vicar Water 84
Distance: Circular, 3km
Terrain: Gravel and loose stone tracks, one ascent. This route is unsuitable for double buggies and less-sturdy four-wheelers.

25. Watermead Country Park 87
Distance: Circular, 6km
Terrain: Surfaced tracks, with a short grass section

26. Wollaton Park 90
Distance: Circular, 3km
Terrain: Surfaced paths

Epics!

27. Birklands and Budby 94
Distance: Circular, 7km
Terrain: Undulating woodland trails and sandy heathland paths

28. Bradgate Hilltops

Distance: Circular, 4.5km
Terrain: Grass tracks with steep ascents and
descents. Recommended for
all-terrain pushchairs only

29. Hemlock Stone

Distance: Circular round Bramcote Hills, and
there and back to Stapleford Park, 3.2km
Terrain: Undulating, loose stone track, may be
muddy when wet. This route contains broad steps.

30. Linacre Reservoirs

Distance: Circular, 3km
Terrain: Woodland tracks. Good footwear
recommended

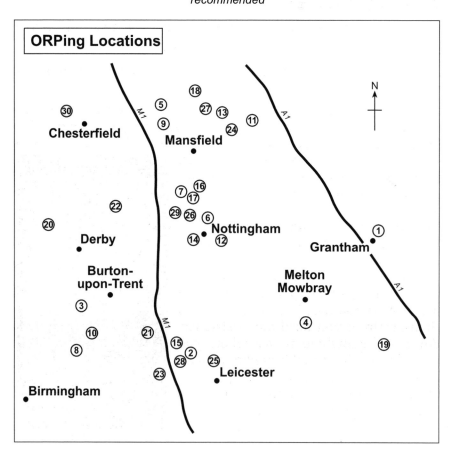

About this Guide

There is a huge variety of routes in this guide from a short walk to a great picnic area with an excellent view, through to more demanding pushchair terrain over tracks that require you to be full of energy! Many of the locations chosen provide ample opportunity to explore further tracks and routes independently. The routes we have chosen are generally just a sample of what these country parks have to offer. So get out there and explore using this guide as an important starting point.

Walk Categories

We have three categories of ORP walks – Amble, Ramble and Epic!

Amble – Ideal if you want an easy, short route

Ramble – A good choice if you want a longer route on more undulating terrain

Epic – A real challenge. These are routes with demanding tracks over difficult terrain – only challenging because you have to drive the pushchair too – but they are excellent fun! So, if you are raring to go with all senses intact, have a sturdy pushchair and good footwear then go for an Epic! Remember that pushing a pram uphill or over rough terrain can be hard work, so we recommend you practice with the easier routes before you attempt any Epic tracks!

The majority of our routes are based on well-trodden paths in popular areas. You will usually see people around or find a shop nearby if you need any assistance. We have highlighted routes where you may have difficulty with double buggies or less-sturdy four-wheelers as we do not want you to begin a walk and become stranded and have to turn back.

Short is just as good as long!

Walk descriptions

For each route you will find a brief italic section describing the location and an outline of what to expect on the walk. In addition, each walk includes details of the location, the distance, the terrain, and the facilities.

Location: Plan ahead. This is fundamental to a good day out. Make sure you know where you are going before you set off. This may sound absurd, but we admit that several times we have left home all flustered, with no idea which direction to turn at the end of the road!

We recommend you carry an Ordnance Survey (OS) map with you at all times for safety. We have listed the Landranger OS map number that you will require, together with the appropriate grid reference to give you the exact location of the site.

Distance: All distances are in kilometres. It's great that you are going to get out there into the countryside, but don't forget that pushing a pram can be hard work. We want you to push that pram, but we don't want you to push yourself too far.

Terrain: The terrain is very important as this will determine your footwear and whether your type of pushchair will withstand the route. We have chosen good tracks for most routes, but if you feel your pushchair or your footwear are not up to the job, please do not attempt it! We want you to enjoy your ORPing routes.

Facilities: Routes are graded on their range of facilities using a star system as follows:

*	=	Car park only
**	=	Car parking and toilets
***	=	Car parking, toilets, visitor centre or information boards, and limited or seasonal refreshments
****	=	Car parking, toilets, visitor centre, wide variety of refreshments available on site. May also include other amenities such as galleries, museums, or gift shops.

Most of the walks we have chosen have a coffee shop/visitor centre or picnic area on site. Where there are no facilities on site, we have noted refreshment opportunities in the vicinity. So treat yourself to a cuppa, you've done really well (after the ORP of course)!

We have not indicated the time each route should take, as this will vary greatly from one ORPer to the next. What may seem an easy route for one individual may be a tough push for another. Time is dependent upon individual fitness, pushchair type, how many people on your walk, the weather, the terrain, whether you stop for a picnic, how long you may spend at the children's play area and so on. However long it takes you is irrelevant – just give yourself a pat on the back for getting out there and ORPing.

Toby checking the route markers are suitable at Poulter Country Park! (walk 9)

Toddle-tastic Sites

Throughout the guide we have noted the "toddle-tastic" locations. These are sites where we found that it was safe to let Toby explore the area (within reason) obviously with supervision, but without the worry of open water or gorse bushes and the like. All the routes are TTT'ed (Toby Tried and Tested) so we hope you have as much fun as we did!

Equipment

Taking yourself out for a walk is easy. Taking a pushchair plus child out to the countryside may seem a daunting experience, but believe me it is just as easy. He will love the fresh air, the views, the new sounds and smells, and gain just as much enjoyment as you, if not more. He may even sleep longer with a mind spinning with new experiences!

For Children

Your little one will generally be facing forwards and receiving the full brunt of the weather, so dress accordingly.

Summer dress

During the summer (we do have one in the Midlands), and even on overcast days, the sun's rays can be incredibly harmful to your child's young and sensitive skin. He should have arms and legs covered, and wear a hat that covers his neck. Also use a sun block suitable for children on any exposed skin. You can buy excellent sun covers or parasols for pushchairs.

Winter dress

It is best to dress your child in several layers of clothing, as this will trap the warmth keeping him all snug. A vest, a sleep suit and an all-in-one fleecy garment are a good choice. You can always add other garments such as an all-in-one waterproof to keep out the wind when you arrive at your ORP route and re-assess the weather. If it's cold, don't forget that his head, hands and feet need to be warm too, as this will keep the rest of his body warm. A winter hat with an under chin popper is a good investment, until he works out how to undo it! Also, gloves attached to a cord will save you time and energy as the little ones love to throw them off, especially when you're crossing puddles.

    Summer or winter, always carry extra garments for your child. Little darlings they are, but they never cease to amaze ...

Several layers of clothing and a footmuff for happy winter ORPing

Accessories

✓ Comfy rucksack to carry accessories

✓ Sun cream (to protect from sun or windburn)

✓ Sunhat or warm hat (depending on weather)

✓ Gloves attached to a cord

✓ Portable nappy changing mat or you could improvise with a coat (preferably someone else's)!

✓ Nappies

✓ Wet wipes

✓ Baby milk and/or food for entire day (be prepared for any eventuality so always carry more than you need)

✓ Spare clothes

✓ Fleece blanket and/or foot muff

✓ Waterproof protection for pushchair

For Adults

You know what to take, but as someone in charge of a child your mind is likely to be focusing elsewhere. Previously, we have left home with numerous outer garments for Toby, and then forgotten our own coats or water bottles! Don't forget to look after yourself. A happy adult equals a happy child!

Beware of Denim – We don't want to lecture but have to write this as we've been caught out ourselves cold and sodden. Try to walk in an alternative to denim. This fabric gets very cold if the temperature is low, and if it rains the fabric against your skin may chafe, and will take hours to dry. You are much better off with a synthetic material such as polyester, fleece, or proper walking trousers.

Accessories

✓ 'Pushchair Paths: East Midlands' – of course!

✓ Appropriate OS Map

✓ Drink

✓ Food

✓ Waterproof/Windproof jacket

✓ Good walking footwear

✓ Gloves, hat, and warm clothing

✓ Sunhat

✓ Sun cream

✓ First aid kit – including medication such as inhalers, antihistamine, anaphylactic shock antidotes for bee stings if required.

Once you have your ORPing bag packed, replenish what you use up in the day and keep it packed and ready for the next excursion.

Safety en route

Many of the routes follow lakeshores, or pass by rivers. We know we don't need to remind you but when the young ones are on the loose please take exceptional care near the water's edge.

Respect the Countryside

You won't be the first person to walk these routes, and neither will you be the last. So, when you're ORPing, remember the following:

✓ Enjoy the countryside but respect it too

✓ Always close gates behind you

✓ Keep dogs under close control

✓ Stay on public paths across farmland

✓ Leave all livestock, crops and machinery alone

✓ Protect wildlife, plants and trees

✓ Take your litter home

Respect all countryside signs!

✓ Be self-sufficient

✓ Prevent all risk of fire

✓ Keep erosion to a minimum

✓ Always carry a map and waterproofs

✓ Keep the noise to a minimum

Finally, give a smile to other ORPers!

The National Forest

🖥 www.visitnationalforest.co.uk

The East Midlands is located in the heart of the UK and although we are incredibly fortunate to have established areas to ORP around such as Sherwood Forest, we are also amazingly lucky to be within the boundaries of the new National Forest. For those who have not heard of this bold environmental project, The National Forest is an unquestionably important initiative to establish "a new Forest for the nation" that is 200 square miles across Leicestershire, Derbyshire and Staffordshire.With over 6 million trees being planted in the last 10 years the forest now provides excellent sites for us to enjoy and explore. As such we have included several ORPing routes in this guide so that you too can get out and see what this bold project has achieved.

The following routes are located within the National Forest:

Walk 2: Bradgate Ruins

Walk 3: Branston Water

Walk 8: National Memorial Arboretum

Walk 10: Rosliston Forestry Centre

Walk 15: Beacon Hill

Walk 21: Sence Valley

Walk 23: Thornton Reservoir

Walk 28: Bradgate Hilltops

ORPing routes at a glance

All routes are circular apart from the "there and back" routes identi-
fied as "T-a-b" in the "Distance" column. Key to facilities (see p2):

*	= Car park only
**	= Car parking and toilets
***	= Car parking, toilets, visitor centre or information boards, and limited or seasonal refreshments
****	= Car parking, toilets, visitor centre, wide variety of refreshments available on site, may also include other interesting amenities such as galleries, museums, or gift shops.

Ambles!

Routes	Distance	Facilities	Features
1. Belton House	2km	****	Stately home; parkland; formal gardens; lake; adventure playground; miniature railway.
2. Bradgate Ruins	5.5km T-a-b	***	Parkland; house ruins; reservoir; crags
3. Branston Water	2km	***	Water park; wildfowl sanctuary; playground
4. Burrough Hill	1.1km T-a-b	**	Iron age hill fort; farm; views
5. Cresswell Crags	1.2km	****	Limestone gorge, crags, caves
6. Highfields Loop	2km	****	Lake, woodland, attractive gardens, boating in summer, arts centre, wildfowl, squirrels, playground
7. Mill Lakes	3.5km	*	Lake, woodland, reedbed, wildfowl, winding engine house
8. National Memorial Arboretum	2km	****	Historic and cultural interest
9. Poulter Summit	2km	*	Hilltop picnic site, views, former colliery site
10. Rosliston	3km	****	Lakes, woodland, reed beds, wildfowl, variety of play areas
11. Rufford Abbey	2km	****	Abbey ruins, lake, woodland, wildfowl, sculptures, gardens, shops, playground
12. Rushcliffe Country Park	3km	***	Parkland, Heritage Steam Museum and trains, playground
13. Sherwood Forest	2km	****	Ancient forest, Major Oak

Rambles!

Routes	Distance	Facilities	Features
14. Attenborough Nature Reserve	5.3km	****	Aquatic nature reserve, wildfowl, woodland
15. Beacon Hill	4km	**	Crags, hilltop, woodland, views, rhododendron maze
16. Bestwood Colliery	2.5km	*	Hilltop, views, winding engine house
17. Big Wood	4km	****	Woodland, views, adventure playground
18. Clumber Lake	5km	****	Lake, woodland, landscaped gardens, wetlands, Gothic chapel, weirs
19. Hambleton Peninsula	7km	***	Lakeshore, woodland, farmland
20. Kedleston Hall	5.3km	****	Stately home, landscaped gardens, woodland, views, weirs, lake
21. Sence Valley	2.3km	**	Parkland, lakes
22. Shipley Circuit	5km	****	Woodland, lakes, water tower, views, adventure and toddler playground
23. Thornton Reservoir	5km	***	Lakeshore, views, dam
24. Vicar Water	3km	****	Hilltop, lakes, view of highest winding gear in country
25. Watermead	6km	***	Aquatic nature reserve, canals, river, locks, weirs, woolly mammoth
26. Wollaton Park	3km	****	Tudor House, deer, lake, playground, museums, gallery

Epics!

Routes	Distance	Facilities	Features
27. Birklands and Budby	7km	***	Woodland, heathland, Major Oak
28. Bradgate Hilltops	4.5km	****	Crags, hilltop, parkland, views, reservoir
29. Hemlock Stone	3.2km T-a-b	*	Ancient stone, woodland, parkland, playground
30. Linacre Reservoir	3km	**	Reservoirs, dams, weirs, woodland

ORPing: a positive experience ...

We hope you will enjoy this guide as much as we have enjoyed writing it – immensely. Parents, grandparents, carers, aunts and uncles, we urge you to get out there and push that pram, whatever the weather. We believe it is really important for children to get fresh air in their lungs and see and experience all that the countryside has to offer.

Why? Well, the experiences they have at any of these locations will broaden their minds because they are just out and about. Their fun day out should help them identify new and exciting things, thus developing their growing vocabulary with "baas", "moos", "duks" and "choo-choos". Not only that, but the toddle-tastic locations and playgrounds may help them develop physically, and for the most positive part, should get them snoring through the night!

Giggles all round as we bumped down the steps while researching routes for this guide – why don't maps indicate steps?

Get yourself and the little ones out from age 0, even if it is just for your sanity! It is excellent fun, and we are sure you won't forget it ...

We hope your little ones have as much fun as Toby has done on his little adventures.

Mel, Antony and Toby

Ambles!

Toddle-tastic Belton House (Walk 1)

1. Belton House

✉ Grantham, Lincolnshire, NG32 2LS

☎ 01476 566116

🖥 www.nationaltrust.org.uk

Just outside Grantham, treat yourself to a day out with fine architecture, extensive parklands, wonderful gardens and sumptuous cream teas, at the National Trust owned Belton House. This ORP route leads you through the grounds of Belton, passing the dazzling Orangery, the delightful formal gardens and the tranquil Boathouse Pond for a taster. Then it's up to you to explore the largest children's adventure playground in Lincolnshire (if you wish), and to take a ride on the miniature railway – this is a great location for any age.

Location: OS Map 130, GR 939394

Distance: Circular 2km

Terrain: Gravel and woodland paths, one lakeshore bridge may be too narrow for double buggies.

Facilities: Car park; toilets; baby changing; tea rooms and restaurant; gift shop; adventure playground; miniature railway; maze (opens 2006); picnic areas.

Note: As this walk takes place on a National Trust property, please check opening times before you go.

The Route

1. From the car park, take the track to the left of Belton House passing the toilets and then entering the yard (the yard is cobbled). Pass the restaurant to your left, and continue straight through the gate in the wall into the formal gardens.

2. Keeping right, pass in front of the fountain, where there are impressive views across the gardens to the Orangery. The track

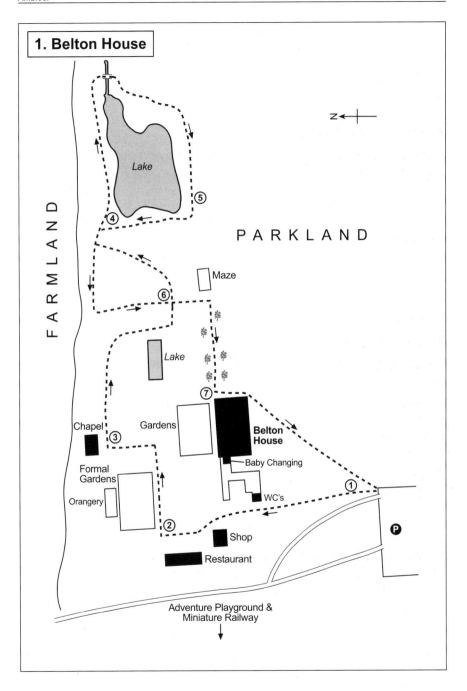

1. Belton House

FARMLAND

Lake

PARKLAND

⑤

④

N

Maze

⑥

Lake

⑦

Chapel ③

Gardens

Belton
House

Baby Changing

Formal
Gardens

Orangery

WC's

②

①

P

Shop

Restaurant

Adventure Playground &
Miniature Railway

The manicured lawns and Orangery of Belton House

leads to steps, but pass to the side up the gentle incline on the grass. Bear left and follow the path down to the chapel.

3. Bear right at the chapel following the path by the large hedge into parkland. Thousands of daffodils flank this track in the spring, so get your glad rags on and be rid of those winter blues with a visit to Belton! The track soon bears right passing a small lake to your right and a seating area to your left. Following the sign to "Lakeside Walk" the path weaves throughout the landscaped gardens to Boathouse Pond.

4. Continue through the gate and follow the self-evident path around the lakeshore, under the canopy of magnificent mature trees.

5. Pass through the next gate and over the bridge (this is a little narrow for double buggies) following the track towards the Boathouse. There is an excellently placed bench by the Boathouse providing sweeping views across the lake. Continue on as the path bears left, and then at the next junction follow the track that

leads to the boundary of the park adjacent to farmland on the right.

6. As the track bears round to the left continue straight until you meet the broad gravel track lined with ornate stone statues. To the left is the maze, and to the right you can see Belton House. Follow the track towards the House.

7. When you reach the House take the track immediately to the left around the House and continue across to the car park.

Note: Belton House has much to offer with 36 acres of gardens and 1,300 acres of Estate. If you fancy getting away from the main areas take a stroll down one of the long estate roads and visit the sheep and deer, or other lakes and woodland areas scattered around the estate. There are some great "toddle-tastic" spots. On one visit we were enjoying a picnic in the grass and Toby was quietly paddling in the puddles along the estate road. Then he decided to sit in the puddle fully clothed. Marvellous – I know we should've known, but there's a first time for everything! Extra clothes are always a must ...

2. Bradgate Ruins

✉ Bradgate Park Trust, Estate Office, Deer Barn Buildings, Bradgate Park, Newtown Linford, Leicester, LE6 0HE

☎ Tel: 0116 236 2713

As Leicestershire's biggest country park, Bradgate has much to offer from the ruins of Bradgate House, to the sweeping Cropston reservoir, the majestic woodland and rolling grasslands. This well-trodden Amble leads you to the ruins of Bradgate House via Cropston Reservoir, and on through woodland and grassland to the facilities at the other end, before you retrace your steps all the way back. The kids will love to cycle this one!

Location: OS Map 129, GR 544114

Distance: There and back 5.5km

Terrain: Surfaced flat path

Facilities: Car park; toilets; tea rooms with gift shop; information centre; picnic area.

The ruins of Bradgate House

The Route

1. Park in Hallgate car park and follow the surfaced track straight ahead by Cropston Reservoir. You will pass the information point and toilets at the southern end of the reservoir.

2. Continue along the track through grassland passing the ruins of Bradgate House to the right of the path.

   This site reveals the ruins of the Tudor house and grounds that were the birthplace of Lady Jane Grey who was Queen of England for nine

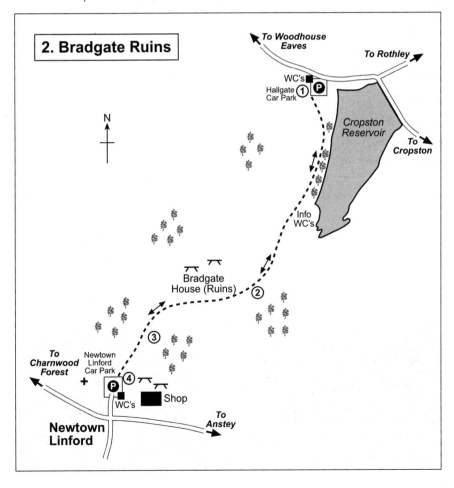

2. Bradgate Ruins

days in 1553. Behind the house are several picnic tables and benches. There is also a small lake here so mind the kiddies.

3. Continue along the track passing crags, streams, woodland and grassland to the Newtown Linford car park. Here you will find a café, gift shop and picnic area.

4. Retrace your steps back to Hallgate car park.

3. Branston Water

✉ Burton-upon-Trent, Staffordshire

Note: We have mischievously stretched the East Midlands borders (only slightly) for this route. Branston Water is located in Staffordshire which is strictly defined as being in the West Midlands, however as it is literally on the Staffordshire/Derbyshire border we could not resist inserting it into this guide so that you can enjoy a day out here! We apologise to any ORPer who takes their borders seriously…

☎ 01283 508573

🖥 www.eaststaffsbc.gov.uk

This pocket of parkland situated adjacent to the Trent and Mersey canal, is a wildlife haven definitely worth a visit. Previously a gravel pit, this area is now a rich aquatic scene accommodating Staffordshire's largest reed bed. The approach to Branston Water Park is quite industrial, but do not let this put you off. As you pass through the gate, you will enter a peaceful wildfowl sanctuary where you can relax and enjoy blackberry picking, or have a picnic. The paths of Branston lead you around the lake and you may extend your route along "The Way for the Millennium" towpath if you fancy a longer walk.

Location: Branston Water Park, OS Map 128, GR 217211

Distance: Circular, 2km

Terrain: Flat, broad, loose stone track

Facilities: Car parking; toilets; visitor centre; children's play area; just outside the water park along the towpath is "The Bridge Inn" pub.

The Route

1. From the visitor centre walk up to Alligator Point for a good viewpoint of the park and surrounding countryside. Toby thought the countless numbers of swans, mallards, and Canada geese were wonderful as he could practise his new-found vocabulary, "duk"!

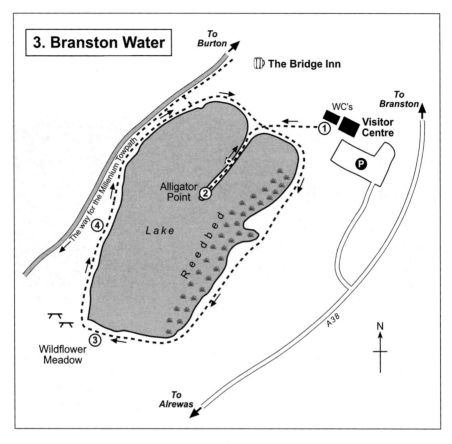

2. Retrace your steps towards the visitor centre and bear right around the lakeshore, passing the reed bed that is spectacular in size, running along most of the length of the lake. If you visit in the summer, this area is teeming with birds and insects.

3. On reaching the southern end of the water, you will find the wild-flower meadow, and picnic area. This is a good place to rest a while and enjoy the views.

4. The ORP along the western lakeshore provides good views of the reed bed opposite.

On the way around look out for other visitors to the park which include

Staffordshire's largest reedbed envelopes half the shoreline of Branston Water
(Walk 3)

waders, oyster catchers, redshank and herons. To the left you will see several tracks linking to the canal towpath. This towpath is "The Way for the Millennium" which will lead you into Burton-upon-Trent. If you fancy some refreshments there is a pub a short walk along to the right.

The route ends at the car park.

4. Burrough Hill

✉ Leicestershire County Council, Burrough on the Hill, Melton Mowbray.

☎ 0116 267 1944

💻 www.leics.gov.uk

Just 5 miles south of Melton Mowbray is Burrough Hill, the site of a large Iron Age Hill Fort. Situated on a marlstone escarpment, this is one of the highest points in Leicestershire at 690 feet above sea level, and if that's not enough to tempt you, you don't have to walk up hill to get to it! The well-preserved ramparts provide an impressive viewpoint of the surrounding area and there is an accompanying toposcope on site.

Location: OS Map 129, GR 766115

Distance: There and back, 1.1km

Terrain: Loose stone and grass track.

Facilities: Car parking; toilets; baby changing.

The Route

1. From the car park continue through the gate along the farm track. Toby loved the tractors, horses, cows and sheep that he saw and was moo-ing and baa-ing for the rest of the day – a very educational ORPing route!

2. At the next gate, pass through and continue across the grass to the site of the fort. If you fancy taking the path down, it is a there-and-back rutted grass

The toposcope and ramparts of Burrough Hill provide an excellent viewpoint

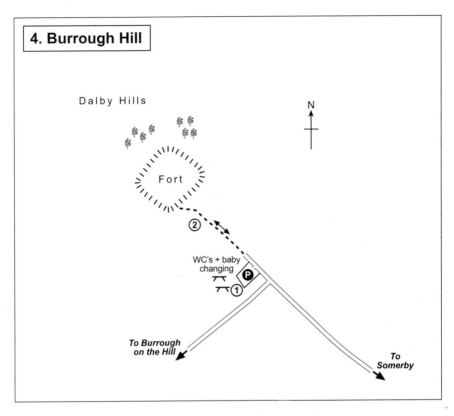

track that loosely leads around the base of the fort.

You will notice the extensive grass area hemmed in by the steep walls of the fort. This is a great toddle-tastic area, but keep an eye on the little ones near the rampart walls. These impressive ramparts provide stunning views across the Dalby Hills.

When you have finished exploring, simply retrace your steps back to the car park.

5. Cresswell Crags

✉ Crags Road, Welbeck, Worksop, Nottinghamshire, S80 3LH

☎ 01909 720378

🖥 www.cresswell-crags.org.uk

Cresswell Crags is an impressive limestone gorge hidden away in the rolling landscape of the Nottinghamshire/Derbyshire border. This Amble follows the foot of the cliffs on either side of the gorge. There are excellent information boards along the route revealing the lives of the Stone Age hunters who inhabited the caves more than 10,000 years ago. Toby could not believe his eyes as he stared at the dramatic sight of the crags towering above – kids and adults alike will love this one.

Location: OS Map 120, GR 538744

Distance: Circular, 1.2km

Terrain: Flat compact path

Facilities: Car park; toilets; visitor centre with refreshments and information; picnic site

The Route

1. From the Visitor centre, follow the sign "To the Crags". There is a gentle path down to a picnic area, followed by a slight incline up to the gorge walk.

2. Bearing left after the gate follow the track beneath the crags, firstly passing the Boat House Cave. This path has gentle undulations.

3. As you reach the western end of the gorge, you will pass the impressive Church Hole Cave. Continue along the self-evident path to the opposite side of the gorge where the track runs parallel to the road.

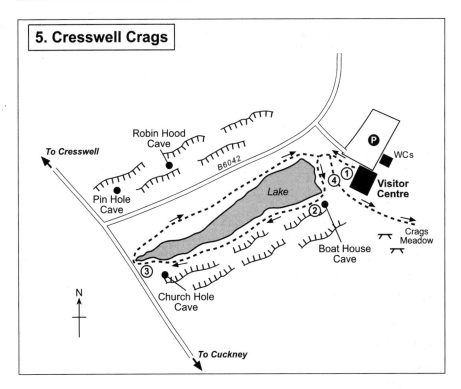

5. Cresswell Crags

To Cresswell

Robin Hood Cave

B6042

Pin Hole Cave

Lake

Boat House Cave

Church Hole Cave

Visitor Centre

WCs

P

Crags Meadow

N

To Cuckney

The information boards along this stretch are very interesting revealing that archaeological digs have found remains of mammoth, woolly rhinoceros, horse, reindeer and bison in Pin Hole Cave.

4. Continue across to Crags Meadow, which is a lovely place for a picnic before you conclude your walk at the visitor centre.

Ice Age tour

The village of Cresswell is far removed from the Ice Age but as you enter the gorge area you are certain to get a taste of what life was like for Neanderthal Man during these times. The gorge is not only dramatic but it is brimming with a wealth of archaeological and geological facts. The caves have unearthed an amazing array of information to help piece together life here 10,000 years ago.

Discover more by indulging in a site tour to learn about the gorge and its inhabitants. There is the Ice Age, the Rock Art and the Cave tours

Pin Hole Cave and surrounding crags

- give the visitor centre a call to find out times before you visit, but these tours are only open to over-fives.

Follow an activity trail with the kids and see if you have the skills to be an Ice Age hunter.

Splash out and bring a fancy picnic to Crags Meadow and enjoy the gorge from a horizontal position!

Muse around the museum and various interesting displays to enhance your knowledge....

You and your kiddies should be budding, knowledgeable archaeological experts by the end of the day! There are all sorts of events in the Cresswell Gorge calendar, so check out the web to see what's going on and get your wheels down there. When you've finished exploring, simply retrace your steps back to the car park.

6. Highfields Loop

✉ Highfields Park, University Boulevard, Nottingham

☎ 0115 9513192 (Arts Centre)

🖥 www.nottinghamcity.gov.uk/highfields

Adjacent to Nottingham University campus, Highfields Park is a haven for wildlife given the variety of habitats from open water to secluded woodland. The Park may be appreciated at any time of the year whether it's high summer with the flowerbeds in full bloom, or it's the depths of winter and the ducks are skating on the ice. There is always something to see and do. The Highfields figure of eight is a great ORP route if you want a relaxing stroll or an afternoon out with the whole family.

Location: OS Map 129, GR 546382

Distance: Circular, 2km

Terrain: Part tarmac, part gravel track, flat with one minor ascent

Facilities: Car park; toilets; baby changing facilities; D.H. Lawrence Pavilion café; children's play area; boating in the summer on the lake; bowls and croquet to watch.

The Route

1. Facing the lake, bear left from the D.H. Lawrence Pavilion passing the boathouse. You will pass under the canopy of mature trees and huge rhododendron bushes.

   To help slow the pace of life, this route is adorned with an endless supply of benches to admire the tranquil views across the water, or enjoy the wonderful floral displays that decorate the lakeside throughout the year. There are also excellent small paths in and out of the bushes for great games of hide-and-seek!

2. When you reach the bridge cross over to the island and you will enter a delightful secluded woodland area.

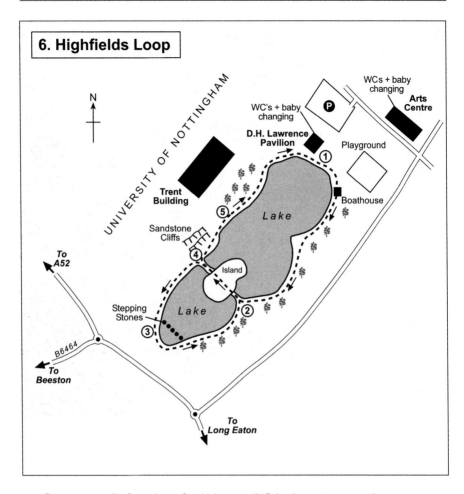

6. Highfields Loop

This is a really fun place for kids – well Toby loves it – as there are often many squirrels darting up and down the trees vying for your attention.

Continue across the island and the next bridge to rejoin the lakeshore path.

3. Bear left towards the stepping-stones at the western end of the lake. Look out for the swans and heron, and look even closer and you may see water vole and kingfisher. Follow the path behind the stepping-stones and walk through the avenue of trees.

4. When you reach the bridge again, cross over, pass through the woodland, but this time turn right onto the northern shore, towards the sandstone cliffs. Wind and rain have weathered these richly coloured cliffs into wonderful cave-like sculptures.

5. The path passes in front of the Trent Building onto a wonderful balcony above the lake, with great views over the surrounding area. Follow the track through woodland before returning to the Lakeside Pavilion.

The track passing below the sandstone cliffs

7. Mill Lakes

✉ The Rangers Office, Alexandra Lodge, Bestwood Country Park, Northern Drive, Park Road, Bestwood Village, Nottingham NG6 8UH

☎ 0115 9273674

💻 www.nottinghamshire.gov.uk

💻 www.greenwoodforest.org.uk

Mill Lakes is an attractive lakeland area to the west of Bestwood Village, and is part of Bestwood Country Park. The park has a great track that circumnavigates the lake through woodland and then by the lakeshore, perfect for ORPers who want a short but scenic walk. There are plenty of opportunities for a picnic or to take the younger kids around on their bike.

Location: Bestwood Country Park, OS Map 129, GR 556476

Distance: Circular, 3.5km

Terrain: Compacted gravel paths with some woodland tracks.

Facilities: Car park only

The Route

1. From Bestwood Village car park bear left around the Winding Engine House. Turn immediately right up the small ascent that leads to a broad track running behind the winding engine house. Follow the track until you reach the "Horse Trail" sign on the right

2. As you pass the "Horse Trail" sign bear right and descend to the next junction, then turn right again into a field. Follow the track across the field towards the information board, and continue through the labyrinth at the far end. Bear immediately left and you will soon join the National Cycle Network track indicated by a large and colourful iron signpost. Follow the sign to Mill Lakes

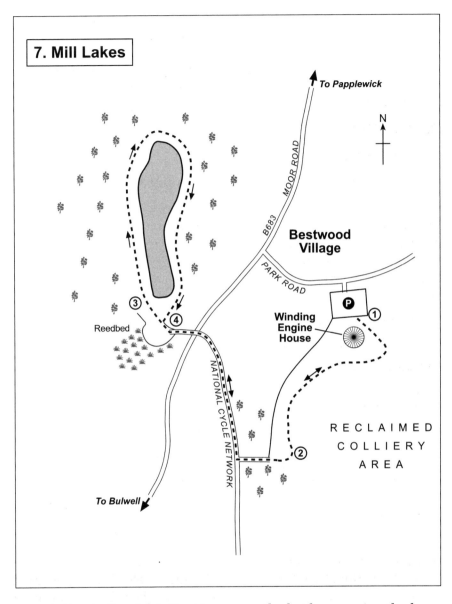

pointing to the right. Continue over the bridge, passing the large reedbed, and into the park.

3. Remain on the broad track around the western lakeside, passing

The track along the western shore of Mill Lakes

through woodland. At the northern end of the lake bear right and continue along the eastern shores.

There are several picnic opportunities along the way and lots of wildfowl to spot. We confess that Toby has not tried and tested the picnic area, as he has been asleep on each picnic visit!

4. When you return to the entrance of the park, retrace your steps back over the bridge, along the cycle route, through the field and bearing left, continue past the winding engine house to the car park.

8. National Memorial Arboretum

⊠ The National Memorial Arboretum, Croxall Road, Alrewas, Staffordshire, DE13 7AR

Note: Like Walk 3, we have stretched the boundaries of the East Midlands very slightly to incorporate this site. It is such an interesting and worthwhile visit that we could not bring ourselves to not include it in this edition. Again this site is on the Staffordshire/Derbyshire border, and although strictly speaking located in the West Midlands, we take full responsibility for placing this Arboretum in our East Midlands Guide. We apologise to any ORPer who takes their borders seriously…

☎ 01283 792333

The National Memorial Arboretum was opened in 2001 on the banks of the River Tame. This Arboretum focuses on groups affected by conflict in the 20th century. With 50,000 new trees and countless interesting plots a visit here will certainly be a thought-provoking experience. ORPing along the broad avenues around plots dedicated to the military, the services, the millennium, victims of conflict and the local area may lead to opportunities for quiet thoughts and reflective moments – this is ORPing with a difference.

Location: National Memorial Arboretum, OS Map 128 GR 182146

Distance: Circular, 2km

Terrain: Flat, broad surfaced or grass trails

Facilities: Car parking; toilets; visitor centre with restaurant, art gallery and gift shop; wheelchair and scooter hire; chapel.

Note: *On our approach to the Arboretum we had envisaged seeing mature trees – well, the name suggests it doesn't it? My initial impulse was to drive straight out of the car park on arrival because there were no trees, well no mature ones anyway. However, I would have been rather foolish had I missed this excellent opportunity to view an incredibly interesting site. Do not be put off by the flat landscape and new trees, go in and have a chat with the knowledgeable staff – I'll eat Toby's socks if you don't find this one interesting!*

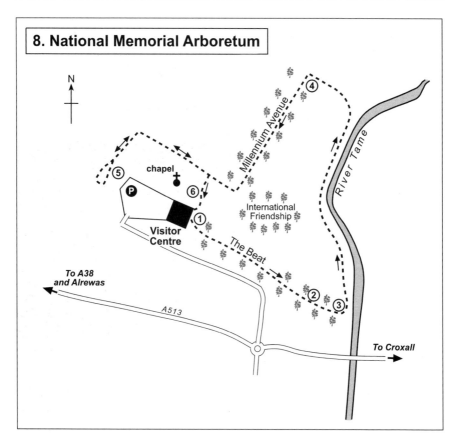

8. National Memorial Arboretum

The Route

1. A good place to begin your tour is at the large statue of a Polar Bear. Toby got really excited when he saw this statue from afar as he thought it was a teddy, but on closer inspection as it towered over him, he began growling at it – perhaps it was not a teddy after all. It is visible from the back of the visitor centre and is dedicated to all who served in the 49th West Riding Infantry Division during the Second World War. To your right, a Police Mutual Assurance plinth marks the start of The Beat, which you should follow towards the River Tame.

2. At the end of The Beat, ORP through the Golden Grove and you will pass a line of Giant Redwoods – which have yet to become giant. An avenue of Purple Beech follows where each tree celebrates the feats of the 29 Victoria Cross winners who served with the Royal Army Medical Corps.

The Polar Bear statue, the starting point of this route

3. On arrival at the banks of the River Tame, bear left along the grass path. After 100m you will pass the haunting 'Shot at Dawn' memorial by Andy DeComyn, which is modelled on Private Herbert Burden. There is a Greek theatre surrounding this statue with names of those who suffered a similar fate. Continue along the riverbank until the path bears left towards the Royal National Lifeboat Institution Plot. You may recognise this plot from the boat resting within.

4. Ahead you will see the large surfaced avenue named Millennium Avenue. Follow this in the direction of the visitor centre. Before reaching the Chapel take the right-hand path along Giffard Avenue. The Avenue is lined with hornbeam hedging and trees.

5. Continue to the Gallipoli plot at the end of Giffard Avenue and retrace your steps back to Millennium Avenue.

6. Continue along St Dunstan's Path to the Garden of Innocence, and the War Widows' Garden. The War Widows Garden is adjacent to the visitor centre, where this route concludes.

9. Poulter Summit

✉ Whaley Road, Nether Langwith, Derbyshire

💻 www.derbyshire.gov.uk

Poulter Country Park is a great find and definitely worth a visit for a grand picnic extravaganza. Located near Nether Langwith, mining country in the land of Robin Hood, the parkland has been created from the spoil tip of the former Langwith Colliery. This is a short walk passing a small lake and reed bed, continuing up to the top of the hill to be rewarded with 360 degree views over the gentle undulating hills of the Derbyshire/Nottinghamshire border. The hilltop is a large expanse of "toddle-tastic" grassland that is a safe place for a family to relax and enjoy a picnic.

Location: OS Map 120, GR525705. From Nether Langwith, use the first car park on the right along Whaley Road.

Distance: Circular, 2km

Terrain: Gravel and grass tracks, one ascent

Facilities: Car park only

An excellently placed bench on the "toddle-tastic" Poulter Summit

The Route

1. Take the track past the two small lakes and a reedbed. Ignoring the sign to Scarcliffe Park continue straight on the path that runs beside the trees that screen you from Whaley Road.

2. Before you reach the gate leading into the car park, bear right up the grass slope to the hilltop. You will pass several green markers that will lead you to the viewpoint at the top where there are four excellently placed benches commanding eye-stretching views across the area.

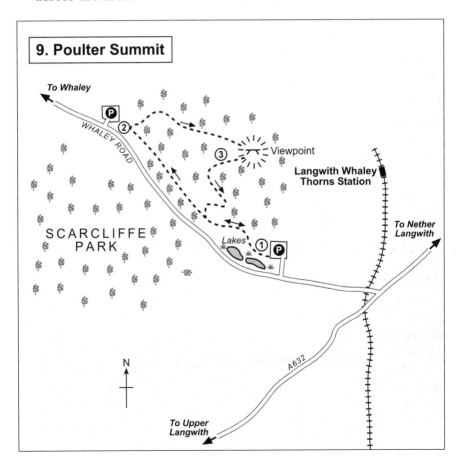

This is "toddle-tastic" country. On one occasion, Toby ran free and picked lots of "wowers" (daisies) for Mummy, which was great until we got home and he picked all the flowers in the garden too!

3. There are many paths to explore around the top, but the simplest way down is to keep following the green markers until the track rejoins the initial gravel path. Retrace your steps bearing left back to the car park.

Note: This ORP route is good to combine with nearby Cresswell Crags. You could tour the Cresswell gorge in the morning and laze around in the afternoon on the tops of Poulter.

10. Rosliston

✉ Rosliston Forestry Centre, Burton Road, Rosliston, Derbyshire, DE12 8JX

☎ 01283 563483

🖳 www.roslistonforestrycentre.co.uk

What a delightful place! Rosliston Forestry Centre opened in 1994, and has a wealth of fun for everyone. There are hay meadows, lakes, reed beds, a bluebell wood, a snowdrop wood, and a wonderful sensory garden. There are a variety of waymarked woodland walks, together with cycle tracks of varying distance, great for young children. These are all waiting to be explored – an excellent day out for the whole family whatever the weather.

Location: OS Map 128 GR 243175

Distance: Circular, 3km

Terrain: Generally flat, broad, loose stone track

Facilities: Car park; toilets; baby changing; visitor centre; indoor soft play area; outdoor adventure playground; cycle hire; crazy golf; fishing; barn shop; wildlife hide; craft shop; restaurant; wheelchair and scooter hire.

The Route

1. From the main entrance, turn left towards Flight Pond. This first section of the ORP passes through larch and broad-leaved woodland, together with Corsican pine. Once at Flight Pond, you are likely to see swans and other resident and migratory wildfowl.

   A fun pastime for kids may be to see if they can spot the different leaf types.

2. Continue to Greenheart Lake. This is a good spot for a picnic – we had one here in January, it was slightly fresh but there was still lots to see. The lake accommodates a large reed bed and in the

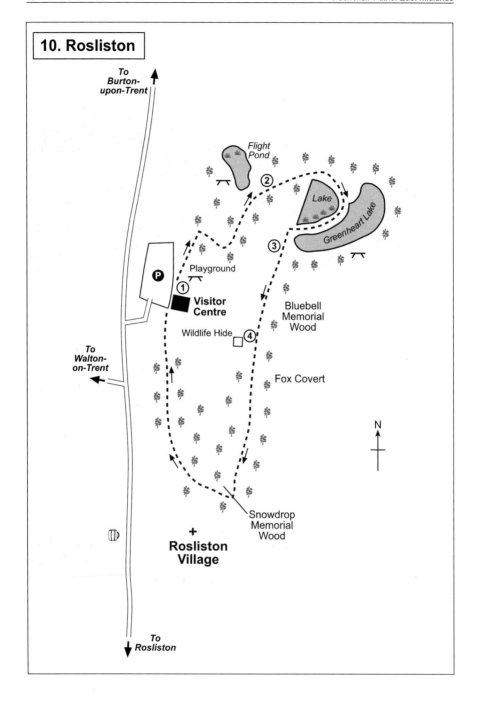

10. Rosliston

To Burton-upon-Trent

Flight Pond

②

Lake

Greenheart Lake

③

Playground

P

①

Visitor Centre

Bluebell Memorial Wood

Wildlife Hide ④

To Walton-on-Trent

Fox Covert

N

Snowdrop Memorial Wood

Rosliston Village

To Rosliston

Greenheart Lake and reedbeds

summer this is rich with birds and insects. There are several benches here so you can rest awhile.

3. Continue towards the Bluebell Memorial Wood. Just before you reach Meadow Pond take the left turning into the Wood. This slight detour will also take you to Fox Covert, which boasts mature broad-leaved woodland. Look out for the rabbits!

4. Retrace your steps back to the path and continue towards the meadows.

    Look out for the large wildlife hide to the right of the path. It is possible (if you are extra lucky) to see kestrels, kingfishers and other field and woodland birds such as skylarks and lapwings feeding here.

Continue ORPing and you will see the spire of Rosliston Village ahead. Passing Snowdrop Memorial Wood the track soon bends to the right, and returns to the visitor centre.

11. Rufford Abbey

✉ Rufford Country Park, Ollerton, Newark, Nottinghamshire
NG22 9DF

☎ 01623 822944

💻 www.nottinghamshire.gov.uk

Rufford is situated in Robin Hood Country and is a fantastic place for a family day out. There is so much to explore and plenty of opportunities to sit back and relax too. Visit the ruins of the 12th century Cistercian Abbey, explore the formal gardens and sculpture collection, discover the secrets of the Orangery, or visit the ice houses and animal graves. There is an excellent ceramics centre to browse round at one end of the lake and a teddy bear shop at the other – something for everyone. This ORPing trail leads you along quiet paths by the lakeshore, through woodland and finally island hops across the lake.

Location: OS Map 120 GR 645648

Distance: Circular, 2km

Terrain: Broad surfaced or gravel track

Facilities: Car park; baby changing facilities; toilets; playground; gallery and ceramic centre; variety of shops; restaurant.

The Route

1. From the car park, you cannot miss the ruins of the Abbey ahead. To the left is a sign directing you to Queen Mother's Walk. Follow this path and it will lead you through a wonderful procession of espalier trees to the lakeside.

2. At the lakeside, bear left where ORPing is easy and flat along the tranquil shores right up to the northern end of the water.

   Constructed in 1750, the lake provided power for a corn mill. These days it is home to an assortment of wildfowl – very entertaining to watch. If you visit in the winter you will see the lake glowing with the rich red of dogwood along the banks.

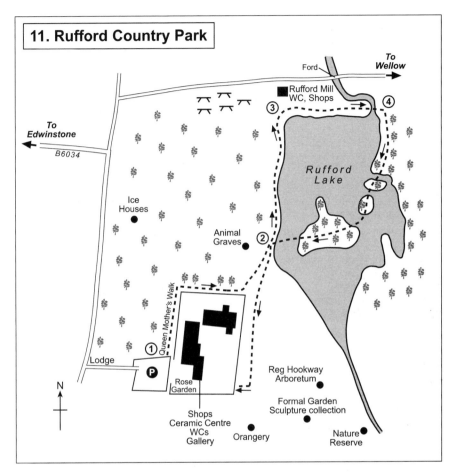

11. Rufford Country Park

3. On reaching the northern end of the lake, you will find Rufford
   Mill, a Garden Shop, an Outdoor Shop, and a quaint teddy bear
   shop.

   There is also a water ford here where it is great fun to watch the cars
   splashing through and drenching anyone in sight. Naughty but nice!

4. From the Mill, cross over the bridge and bear right into Scotland
   Bank Wood – look out for the squirrels darting around. This track
   links the islands in the lake leading you back to the western
   shoreline. Here we will leave you to explore the rest of the park as
   there's so much to see ...

Interesting sculptures inside the Cistercian Abbey ruins

Other areas to discover at Rufford:

✓ Wander the formal gardens that are overflowing with colour in the summer.

✓ Chill out in the Reg Hookway Arboretum.

✓ Take a push around the sculpture collection, interesting in its diversity from the classic to the contemporary. These will appeal even to the very young as there are some colourful and intriguing designs on show.

✓ The Orangery is definitely worth a visit. In 1730 this area was a bathhouse. What a unique and unusual building with a remarkable history.

✓ To complete your day, pamper yourself at the restored Victorian kitchen of the Abbey – there's bound to be something on the menu to wet your appetite.

12. Rushcliffe Country Park

✉ Mere Way, Loughborough Road, Ruddington, Nottingham, NG11 6JS

☎ 0115 9215865

🖥 www.rushcliffe.gov.uk/countrypark

Previously the Ministry of Defence Ordnance and Survey depot, Rushcliffe Country Park established itself in the 1990s with woodland, grassland and wildflower meadow together with a lake area and reed bed. The adjacent Transport Heritage Centre has engines running seasonally and various attractions throughout the summer. The park is a gift for ORPing as the trails are relatively flat and broad and there are many to explore.

Location: Map 129 GR 576323

Distance: Circular, 3km

Terrain: Broad, smooth gravel track, flat with one minor ascent

Facilities: Car park; toilets; information centre; children's playground and skateboarding area; refreshments by playground (summer only); Nottingham Transport Heritage Centre; Ruddington has a whole host of amenities, and you can walk into the village from the country park.

The Route

1. From the main car park, follow signs to the lake. Keeping to the left along the lakeshore, you are sure to see moorhens, coots, mallards, grebes and swans. This is a great place for a picnic and there are several well-placed benches and picnic tables.

2. Pass the reed bed and follow the sign to "Wildflower Meadows". After 200m you will reach a T-junction with the wildflower meadow ahead.

   This area hosts a succession of summer flowers that attract many butterflies and bees. If you know your wild flowers you will recognise knapweed, yellow rattle and many ox-eye daisies.

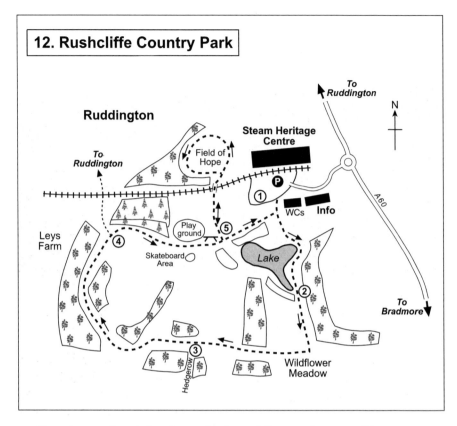

12. Rushcliffe Country Park

3. Keeping to the right along the broad flat track you will soon come across an ancient boundary hedgerow dating back to 1699. Continue straight and ignoring any tracks to the right you will soon see a large fenced off plantation.

At the next fork, bear left around the plantation and follow the track up a gentle incline to the corner of the woodland area to reach a sweeping view over the Gotham and East Leake Hills. The path then descends between plantations before heading up to a small hillock. This top reveals good views over Ruddington.

4. Turn right towards the children's play area where you will find something for all ages.

There is a great playground for the young ones, for the older kids there

The great ORPing tracks along the western corner of the park

is a large skateboarding ramp and kite-flying area, and for the adults there is ample space to laze around or have a game of frisbee.

5. To the right of the playground, take the path over the bridge. The bridge is an excellent observation point over the Heritage Centre. After the bridge the path leads into the Field of Hope where you can complete a loop around the parkland area. Return over the bridge and follow signs back to the car park.

The Nottingham Transport Heritage Centre

💻 www.nthc.co.uk

Located adjacent to the country park, this is home to the Great Central Railway, and is a super addition to an ORPing walk. The Heritage Centre accommodates a large collection of road and rail transport vehicles and a large model railway. From Easter until late October the gates are open and you can jump onto a steam train for a trip down the tracks.

13. Sherwood Forest

✉ Sherwood Forest Country Park, Edwinstowe, Mansfield,
Nottinghamshire NG21 9HN

☎ 01623 823202

💻 www.nottinghamshire.gov.uk

The Major Oak

Among the most popular spots in the East Midlands, Sherwood Forest Country Park is truly a gem for ORPers with its excellent broad tracks through ancient woodland and heathland. Of course, the main reason most visitors come is to feast their eyes on The Major Oak. Spectacularly large at 10m wide and with a 28m spread of branches, it is quite a sight. This route leads you to the Oak and back through some spectacular mature woodland.

Location: Sherwood Forest Country Park, OS Map 120 GR 626676

Distance: Circular, 2km

Terrain: Flat broad paths, circular

Facilities: Car park; toilets; baby changing; exhibition centre; heritage shop; restaurant.

In summer the Park is very popular, particularly when it's The Robin Hood Festival (www.robinhood.co.uk/robinhood) in August. You can go back in time and enjoy a fun packed week of mediaeval merriment for all the family. As the gates are open all year, you could also visit on a crisp winter day when the ancient oaks are glistening in the winter sunshine. They are an amazing sculptural sight. If only they could talk, and tell their story...

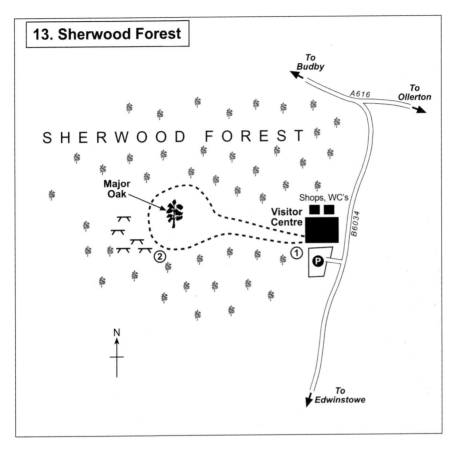

13. Sherwood Forest

The Route

1. This classic walk for the whole family begins outside the visitor centre. Follow the blue marked posts in a clockwise direction.

2. After half a mile, you will see the sign "5 minutes to the Major Oak" – nearly there!

Passing through oak woodland, keep an eye out for the really ancient trees. They are magnificent. As you round the corner the amazing sight of the 800-year-old, 23-tonne "guardian of the forest" awaits.

When Toby first saw this ancient tree he was eager to share the experience with Teddy, who was also suitably impressed. There are well-situated picnic tables in this area for you to rest awhile and enjoy the spectacle.

Follow the waymarked signs back to the visitor centre and car park.

Out and about in the Sherwood Forest area

As this "Amble!" is a short walk you may wish to combine it with a little extra...

Edwinstowe is a short wander through the forest. You could grab a cuppa in the High Street by the bronze statue of Robin Hood and Maid Marian. Legend has it that this famous couple wed in the parish church here.

Ollerton is a short drive away and with a watermill to show the kids, it's sure to be a hit! You could also treat yourself in the Watermill Tea Shop, (which won the Tea Council Award 2005) with a fine Earl Grey and a slice of homemade cake.

As it's not always about having a cuppa and a slice of cake you could combine this walk with another ORP in the area such as Walk 9: Poulter Summit, or Walk 11: Rufford Abbey.

Rambles!

Rambling Dads at Attenborough Nature Reserve (Walk 14)

14. Attenborough Nature Reserve

✉ Barton Lane, Attenborough, Nottingham, NG9 6DY

☎ 0115 9721777

🖥 www.broxtowe.gov.uk/index/tourism

Located in the attractive Trent Valley on the south-western fringe of Nottingham, Attenborough is designated a Site of Special Scientific Interest. With secluded woodland tracks, lush waterside sanctuaries, sweeping views of the River Trent, and a fantastic Fair Trade café what more could you want? Take a trip to the Reserve and enjoy the network of paths that run between the lakes and through the woodlands.

Location: OS Map 129, GR 516339.

Distance: Circular, 5.3km

Terrain: Flat compact paths, potential to be muddy in wet weather

Facilities: Car park; visitor centre with gift shop, toilets, baby changing, information.

The Route

1. Opposite the visitor centre, and located in the car park is a large wooden signpost where you should follow the sign to "Attenborough Village". Ignoring tracks to the left, keep right until you reach the northern end of Tween Pond.

2. Cross the small bridge and follow the track past the cricket ground into Attenborough Village. Following the signs "Bridleway to Meadow Lane" the route leads you along "The Strand" passing lovely Victorian houses, a cricket and adjacent football pitch (on your right) and then, as the road narrows, it leads to a track as you re-enter the Reserve.

3. Continue along the causeway – this route is a bridleway so beware of cyclists and horse riders – looking out for the extensive

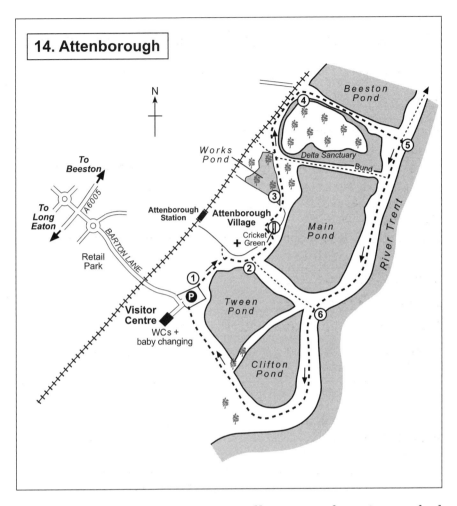

blackberry picking sites. You will soon reach an iron-arched bridge that commands an excellent view over the reserve. Keeping left after the bridge and still following signs "Bridleway to Meadow Lane" you will follow a quiet woodland track which soon runs parallel to the railway line.

4. When you reach the railway crossing bear right along the North Path track signposted "River Trent and Beeston Marina".

5. Bear right along the riverside path following signs "Riverside

The bridge crossing provides great views and time for a natter

Path to Trent Lock". This path has an excellent vantage point across the floodplain where you can see the small village of Barton-in-Fabis and surrounding farmland, together with mature weeping willows reclining into the meandering path of the river. In the autumn, be ready to collect your pie filling as a mass of blackberry bushes line the path.

6. Continue around Clifton Pond which is a delightful stroll along the riverside path. Follow signs marked "Attenborough Nature Centre" and you will eventually arrive back at the visitor centre and car park.

15. Beacon Hill

✉ Beacon Hill Country Park, near Woodhouse Eaves, Loughborough

☎ 01509 890048

🖳 www.leics.gov.uk

Located south of Loughborough, Beacon Hill is the second highest point in Leicestershire. The summit is the site of a Bronze Age Hill Fort, which is an Ancient Monument protected by English Heritage. Keep an eye out, as there are rare breeds of sheep and alpacas grazing in the area. This ORPing route leads you through wonderful woodland together with a secret rhododendron maze (sshh – don't tell anyone), to a panoramic view on the summit. For the East Midlands this is a fabulous summit push, to get those thighs pumping.

Location: OS Map 129 GR 522148

Distance: Circular, 4km

Terrain: Loose stone track, with one ascent to Beacon Hill

Facilities: Car park; baby changing facilities; toilets; native tree collection; refreshments can be found in nearby Woodhouse Eaves, or there is an excellent Organic Home Farm near Buck Hill (OS 505166) which has scones as big as an adult hand, and a children's farm area to explore in the summer.

The Route

1. From the waymarked signs in the lower car park follow the walkers route (indicated by a boot) that leads you along a gravel path into woodland. Soon you will see a fun detour to the left into a secret rhododendron maze. This follows a circular route on a large boardwalk – take care if it is wet as the path may be slippery. The maze will deliver you back to the main track where you plunge into mature mixed woodland.

2. Slowly climbing through the woods, you near the upper car park

..rea. Focus carefully on the trees around and spot the twisted branches - there are some weird and wonderful sculptures.

3. The approach to the summit isn't tough but will get the thighs pumping, and if you are pushing the pram its great for bum toning too! At the top there is a toposcope, and a very well-situated bench.

On one ORPing trip, sharp-eyed Toby spotted an eagle with its trainer. We were transfixed as the eagle swooped majestically from the trainer's arm onto different crags on the hilltop only to rise again and repeat the same trick. Keep your eyes peeled!

4. Continue around the hilltop and to the right of the track you will see a volcanic crag face that is 700 million years old. The path slowly descends into wood-land towards the lower car park, and as you push look out for the carved tree stumps in the woods – there are some intriguing shapes.

5. If you have time, there is a short extension to the Native Tree Site near the lower car park.

Here you will find an interesting commentary on over 20 native British trees. Alternatively, visit this area before your walk, and see if you can spot the trees on the Ramble!

A peaceful Beacon Hill summit

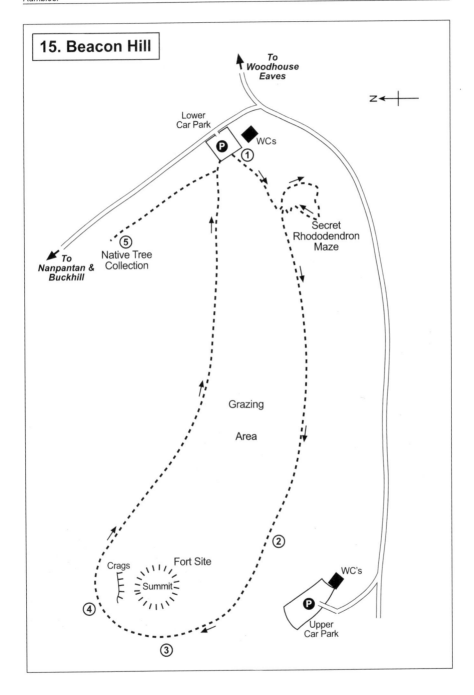

15. Beacon Hill

To Woodhouse Eaves

Z

Lower Car Park

WCs

①

To Nanpantan & Buckhill

⑤ Native Tree Collection

Secret Rhododendron Maze

Grazing

Area

②

Crags Fort Site

Summit

④

③

WC's

Upper Car Park

16. Bestwood Colliery

✉ The Rangers Office, Alexandra Lodge, Bestwood Country Park, Northern Drive, Park Road, Bestwood Village, Nottingham, NG6 8UH

☎ 0115 9273674

💻 www.nottinghamshire.gov.uk

💻 www.greenwoodforest.org.uk

Bestwood Colliery is part of the large green expanse that is Bestwood Country Park. Although the colliery is no longer in existence there remains a wealth of visible history in the area. The colliery was one of the largest in the country and as such it has a huge spoil heap to match, although thankfully this is now a site for nature and leisure. The large winding engine house remains and you may detect the smell of coal in the air. The route begins at the winding engine house and heads up through woodland to the summit of the former spoil heap, leading to panoramic views and great picnic sites.

Location: OS Map 129, GR 556476

Distance: Circular, 2.5km

Terrain: Compact paths with some grass tracks. Steep ascent to the summit.

Facilities: Car park, refreshments and facilities can be found at Bestwood Lodge

---

The Route

1. From the car park bear left around the Winding Engine House and continue along the compact flat track ahead.

2. Following signs to Big Wood the track soon bears left into the woods and then bends to the right where a steep ascent through silver birch woodland begins. Look out for the monkey bumps

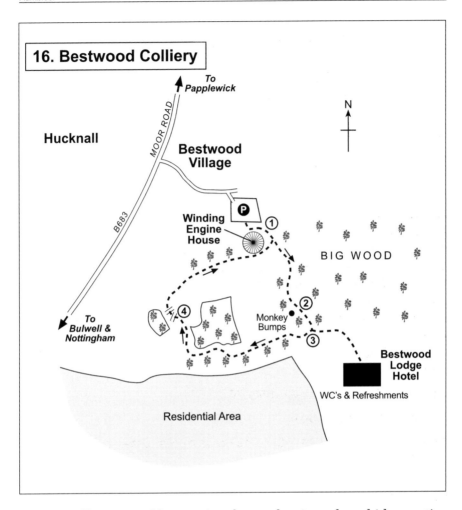

(area of lumps and bumps in a forest clearing where kids practise biking skills) to the right of the track, to get your bearings.

3. When you reach the top, bear right along a narrow track onto the broad grassland area of the summit, where you will be rewarded with extensive views over Big Wood, Top Valley, Bestwood Village and beyond.

Follow the path through the grassland towards the fenced plantation. Cross a gravel track and keeping to the left of the plantation

The Winding Engine House of the former Bestwood Colliery.

you will soon join another track that winds around the south-western corner of the hill.

4. After the path descends, pass through two gates and then bear immediately right. When you reach the "Horse Trail" sign, keep right and follow the track back to the Winding Engine House.

17. Big Wood

✉ The Rangers Office, Alexandra Lodge, Bestwood Country Park, Northern Drive, Park Road, Bestwood Village, Nottingham, NG6 8UH

☎ 0115 9273674

💻 www.nottinghamshire.gov.uk

💻 www.greenwoodforest.org.uk

Big Wood is part of Bestwood Country Park, a green heart in the midst of suburbia. These woods were once part of the most southerly reaches of Sherwood Forest and used to be a royal hunting preserve – an area steeped in history. This route begins at the attractive Lodge and leads you on a circular tour of Big Wood – a lovely walk at any time of the year.

Location: OS Map 129, GR 572465

Distance: Circular, 4km

Terrain: Compact woodland paths and surfaced road

Facilities: Car park at the Lodge, refreshments at Bestwood Lodge Hotel (0115 9203011 / www.bw-bestwoodlodge.co.uk), adventure playground.

The Route

1. At Bestwood Lodge Hotel, continue up the lodge road passing by woodland and playing fields before you reach the sign to Big Wood.

2. Pass through the gate into Big Wood and bear left along Woodmans Path. This is a broad undulating track that leads around Big Wood. Look out for the Horse Trails as these are well-utilised, much to Toby's amazement.

On one visit Toby was speechless as these huge animals passed in front of his pushchair – we have since taken him to see many horses in the hope that we get a similar reaction each time!

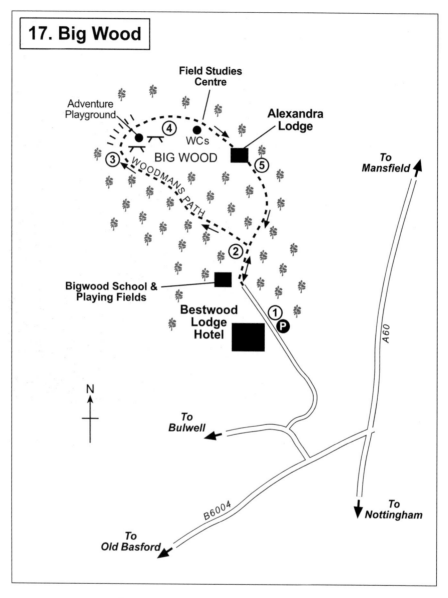

3. Continue until you reach the adventure playground. The playground is a great spot for a picnic commanding excellent views over Nottinghamshire and the winding engine house below – see

"Bestwood Colliery" Ramble (Walk 16) for a closer look at the engine house.

4. Keeping to the Path, bear right into woodland and descend to the field studies centre and toilets.

   If you peer into the woods near the facilities, there is a large carved archway hidden in the bushes, which is quite impressive.

5. Continue along Main Drive and you will soon come to Alexandra Lodge, an architecturally impressive archway.

Hitching a lift in Big Wood

Remain on Main Drive all the way back to Bestwood Lodge Hotel and the car parking area, following the waymarked signs.

18. Clumber Lake

✉ Clumber Park Estate Office, Clumber Park, Worksop,
Nottinghamshire, S80 3AZ

☎ 01909 544917

💻 www.nationaltrust.org.uk

Clumber Park is an all seasons location. Whether you stroll around the landscaped gardens in the summer, or enjoy a crisp lakeside walk in winter, this is a great place for a day out. The route passes through the landscaped gardens, woodland and wetland, past Hardwick village and over the classical Clumber Bridge – a picturesque ramble for all the family.

Location: OS Map 120 GR 625745

Distance: Circular, 5km

Terrain: Woodland tracks

Facilities: Car parking, baby changing facilities, toilets, excellent tea-rooms, gift shop, cycle hire, plant shop, organic kitchen garden, and conservation centre.

The Route

1. From the tearooms, take the woodland path through the land-scaped gardens towards Ash Tree Hill Wood. The gardens are "toddle-tastic" and great for a game of hide-and-seek. The track begins behind the Gothic chapel and eventually leads to an arch-way which precedes the entry into the Woods.

2. After the archway, keep the fenced woodland to your left and follow the path to the right of the woods. This track leads you around the edge of the woods and then joins the lakeshore.

3. Cross the bridge and follow the broad track bearing right along the lakeshore. Keep an eye out for cormorants, heron, swans, coots, grebes and mallards on these shores. This track leads you past Hardwick village.

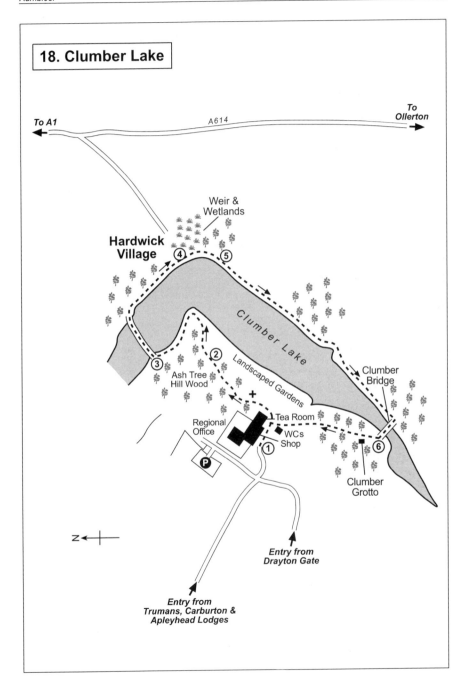

18. Clumber Lake

To A1

A614

To Ollerton

Weir & Wetlands

Hardwick Village

④ ⑤

Clumber Lake

③ ② Landscaped Gardens

Ash Tree Hill Wood

Clumber Bridge

Tea Room

Regional Office

WCs Shop

① ⑥

P

Clumber Grotto

N

Entry from Drayton Gate

Entry from Trumans, Carburton & Apleyhead Lodges

The southern lakeshore track, with Hardwick village in the background

4. Crossing the next bridge and weir, you will see a large wetland area to the left of the track with a huge reed bed.

This is a lovely place to stop for a picnic, as there are extensive views in all directions, and several well-placed benches.

5. Continue along the path by the lakeshore, through woodland and grassland, until you reach the classical Clumber Bridge built in 1770.

6. Cross the bridge and take the first right into the woodland again. Pass Clumber Grotto and you will soon be back at the tea rooms near the car parking area, hopefully in time for a cream tea.

19. Hambleton Peninsula

✉ Rutland Water Tourist Information, Sykes Lane, Empingham

☎ 01572 653026

This is a track made for ORPers! Hambleton Peninsula is located on Rutland Water, a huge man-made lake created in the 1970s to meet the rising demand for water in the East Midlands. The peninsula was thankfully spared from flooding as it now provides tranquil shores to stroll around with ever-changing views. This circuit begins at the end of the peninsula, where you firstly ramble the eastern shore along a broad undulating path. There is a mid-point visit to the village of Upper Hambleton where you may stop for a bite to eat and then continue to the western shore and return through pockets of woodland to the peninsula end. This is a lovely circuit and excellent for a day out in any season.

Location: Rutland Water, OS Map 141, GR 925066

Distance: Circular, 7km

Terrain: Loose stone track, broad and undulating

Facilities: Car parking at the peninsula end; refreshments and toilets in the pub in Upper Hambleton, or alternatively you can go to the Nature Reserve Centre at Egleton (a short drive away) that has refreshment facilities, a gift shop and toilets.

Note: There are numerous cattle grids along this route but you can pass through the gates to the side of all of them.

The Route

1. From the peninsula car parking area, bear left along the broad track that descends towards the shore. The path undulates through farmland and woodland and provides sweeping views across the water before leading you up to Upper Hambleton village.

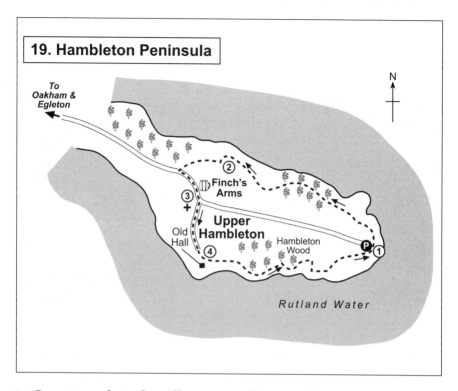

19. Hambleton Peninsula

2. On approach to the village you will notice houses peeking over the hillside across the fields.

This is a lovely spot for a picnic as the waves are lapping on the shores, and the birds are singing in the trees – you could be on the Mediterranean on a sunny day (with your eyes closed)!

The track bears left up the hill, which is a reasonably steep push. You will then have to bear left again and follow the road for 100m into Hambleton Village. There is no pavement so take care, although the motorists seem used to walkers on this part of tarmac as they tend to drive slowly.

3. In Upper Hambleton Village you will pass The Finch's Arms to the left, a great place to stop for a bite to eat. Cross the road, and follow the "No Through Road" sign to the right, down to the lakeshore. You will pass some quaint cottages along the route.

The broad track along Hambleton peninsula

4. Pass by The Old Hall and continue along the lakeshore track through Hambleton Wood. This is attractive mature woodland with an abundance of primroses and bluebells in the spring. The track continues by the lakeshore through pockets of woodland, and leads you to the peninsula end.

20. Kedleston Hall

✉ Derby, DE22 5JH

☎ 01332 842191

🖥 www.nationaltrust.org.uk

The National Trust owned Kedleston Hall is hidden amongst the rolling hills of Derbyshire. The Hall is a grand old stately home, and the grounds are a wonderful mixture of habitats from woodland to landscaped gardens and open water. This is a delightful woodland walk with stunning views of both the estate and the surrounding countryside.

Location: OS Map 128, GR 312403

Distance: Circular, 5.3km

Terrain: Compact gravel paths with some woodland and grass tracks.

Facilities: Car park, restaurant, gift shop, toilets, baby-changing facilities.

Note: As this walk takes place on a National Trust property please check opening times before you go.

The Route

1. Make your way to the gift shop, located to the rear of the ground floor of the Hall, behind the restaurant. From outside the gift shop with the grand staircase to your left, bear right through the landscaped gardens towards the car park.

1a. If the gift shop is closed you may also access the walk from the car park. You will see a sign for "Long and Short walks" on the Hall side of the car park. This leads down to some steps, which you have to traverse to reach the formal gardens. It is not advisable if you are on your own, but of course if there's more than one adult, this route is certainly passable.

20. Kedleston Hall

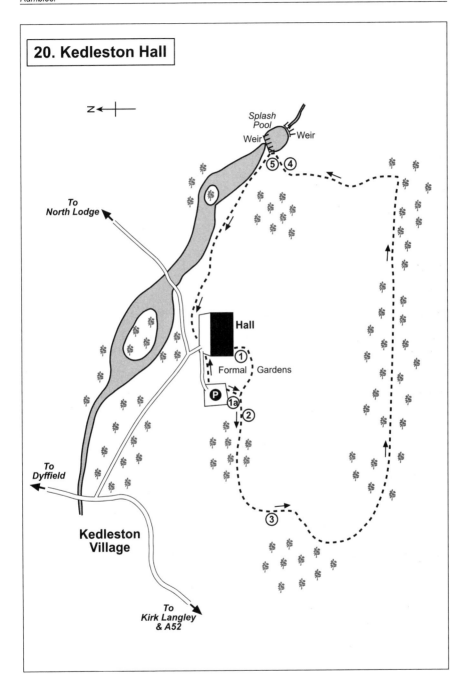

2. Continue through the large iron gate and follow the gravel path past huge rhododendron bushes and magnificent mature trees. There is a gentle ascent to the ridgetop with extensive views over the surrounding countryside.

   Spring is a great time to visit as hundreds of daffodils line this path.

3. Continue through the woodland along the meandering path following the "Long Walk" signs. We thoroughly enjoy this section as vibrant birdsong and squirrels darting in and out of the trees have accompanied us on our way. When you reach the gate, continue ahead to the opposite side of the field. Pass through a second gate and continue on through the woods.

4. As the path descends towards the lake follow the sign to "Splash Pool". The path bears right through the trees to a large weir at the end of the lake.

   The Splash Pool area is an engaging spot as the water from

Follow the signs!

   the huge lake passes into the splash pool, then over another weir to continue downstream through the woods.

5. From the Splash Pool, continue through the gate and follow the lakeshore through parkland keeping left as you reach the boundary of Kedleston Hall. Continue in front of the Hall back to the car parking area.

21. Sence Valley

✉ Ravenstone Road, Ibstock, Leicestershire

☎ 01889 586593

🖥 www.forestry.gov.uk

Sence Valley Forest Park was opened in 1998 after the site was established with nearly 100,000 trees as part of The National Forest. This is a peaceful park, providing a great place to get away from it all. Formerly a disused opencast working, the site has been transformed into a lake and woodland area thriving with wildlife.

Location: OS Map 129 GR 401115

Distance: Circular, 2.3km

Terrain: Flat, broad, loose stone track.

Facilities: Car parking, picnic area, toilets. Amenities in nearby Ibstock

---

Note: There are many paths to investigate at Sence Valley however some of the footpaths and bridges have narrow entrances and gates, not suitable for larger 3-wheelers or double buggies.

The Route

1. From the car park follow the road down to the disabled car park and bear left around the southern shores of Horseshoe Lake.

1a. If you don't wish to follow the road down, you can descend to the Lake via the bridleway at the western end of the car park, but there are some large steps that you will have to carry the pushchair over.

2. At the western end of Horseshoe you will see Goss Lake come into view as you round the corner. (Goss Lake is worth a push around but unfortunately it is a there-and-back route as, at the time of writing, there was no circular pushchair route to be found). Cross the bridge between the two lakes and follow the broad gravel path

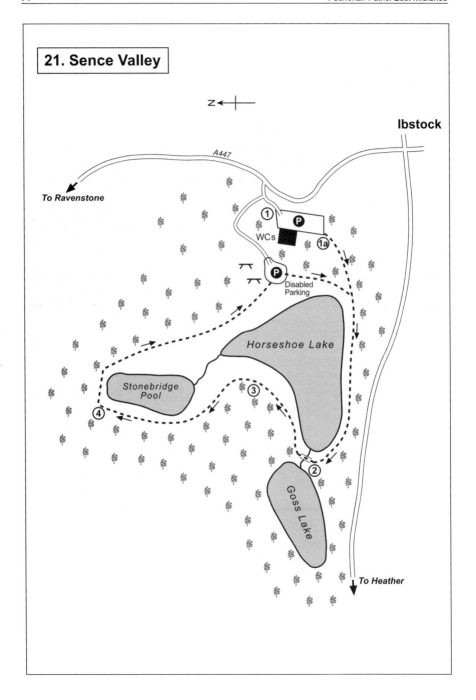

21. Sence Valley

The bridge between Horseshoe and Goss Lakes

along the northern shore of Horseshoe Lake to the right of the plantation.

3. As you approach the end of the plantation you will see several bridges in the grassland. Bear left on the track through the grassland to cross the bridges, and continue along the path through woodland adjacent to Stonebridge Pool.

   On one visit, Toby made me cross the bridges time and time again as he was enthralled by the rumbling noise the wheels made as it crossed the wooden boards. I suggest a game of pooh sticks instead if your little one exudes the same interest in wooden planks – or you'll be there for hours!

4. When you reach a T-junction, turn right and continue around Stonebridge Pool. Pass through the disabled car park, and follow the road back up the hill to the main car park.

Pick Your Own?

✉ Cattows Farm, Swepstone Road, Heather, Leicestershire, LE67 2TD

☎ 01530 260287

Location: OS Map 128 GR 383115

If you are out in the Valley in the summer why not combine an ORP walk with a visit to Cattows Farm, and pick your own seasonal fruit and vegetables? Located just west of Sence Valley Park this family-run business has a selection of seasonal fruit and vegetables and delicious home-grown asparagus. Admission is free so just give them a call to check opening times.

22. Shipley Circuit

✉ Slack Lane, Heanor, Derbyshire, DE75 7GX

☎ 01773 719961

Shipley is a fantastic park for ORPers as the paths are mostly broad and surfaced; there are short and long routes and lots to see and do. This route visits lakes, Shipley Hill and the old water tower, and follows delightful tracks through woodland and grassland. Shipley is a great venue for picnics, a spot of kite flying, or a gentle cycle ride.

Location: OS Map 129, GR 432454

Distance: Circular, 5km

Terrain: Surfaced paths and bridleways, some woodland paths

Facilities: Car park; toilets; café; toddlers playground; adventure play area; trim track; cycle hire.

The Route

1. From the car park, follow the signs to Osbournes Pond but beware as we are taking a short detour before reaching the Pond! Take the first right along the track and enter into Cinderhill Coppice. Bear left around the coppice and spot the weird and wonderful woodcarvings along the way. Taking the first left out of the coppice, bear left again down to Osborne's Pond.

2. Bear right along the lakeshore. Pass through the gate at the end, and continue right along the bridleway named Shipley Lane towards Shipley Hill.

3. When you reach Derby Lodge bear left following the signs to Nottingham Lodge (which we do not visit, but just continue in the direction of). Designed by William Tapper, the identical lodges were built as gatehouses in 1911.

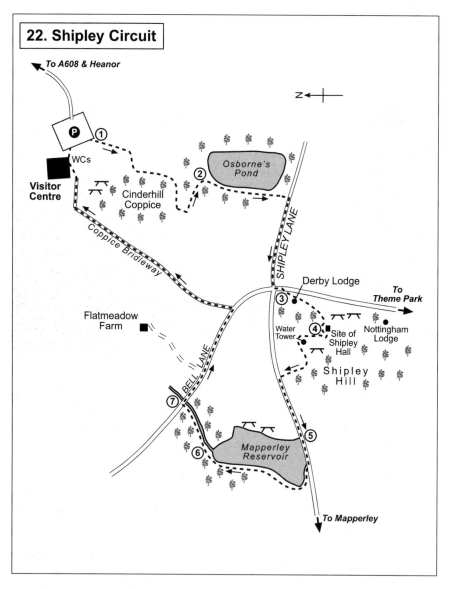

22. Shipley Circuit

To A608 & Heanor

WCs

Visitor Centre

Cinderhill Coppice

Osborne's Pond

Coppice Bridleway

SHIPLEY LANE

Derby Lodge

To Theme Park

Flatmeadow Farm

Water Tower

Site of Shipley Hall

Nottingham Lodge

Shipley Hill

BELL LANE

Mapperley Reservoir

To Mapperley

After a short incline, bear right at the next fork and you will arrive at the car park and site of Shipley Hall – a perfect spot for a picnic. All that is left of the Hall is the outline of the ground floor rooms laid out in the gardens, as the house was demolished in 1943.

The water tower on Shipley Hill, now a private residence

4. From the car park follow Beech Walk to the water tower. About 100m after the water tower bear right through woodland to join Shipley Lane again. Bearing left along the bridleway, continue down to Mapperley Reservoir.

5. Cross the dam wall and bear immediately right along the woodland track. Double buggies may have trouble at the narrow gate to this track. This is a gentle woodland path with grazing land to your left, and birdsong above.

6. Keeping to the left through the wood, when you see the marker "37P" on the left of the track, keep left and follow the footpath to Bell Lane, with the stream to the right of the track.

Please be astute on this section, as on my first visit I took the wrong path and ended up on a very muddy bridleway. The wheels were so caked in mud that when I saw the wonderfully flat gravel footpath on the opposite side of the stream I impulsively decided to cross the stream instead of turning back. Needless to say I was a wet-footed irresponsible Mummy. Please do as I say, not as I do!

7. On reaching Bell Lane bear right and continue past the turn to Flatmeadow Farm until you reach Coppice Bridleway, the next turning to the left. Follow this track back to the visitor centre. Do not be tempted to take a shortcut via Flatmeadow Farm as you will reach a stile and a padlocked gate – not good for the ego!

23. Thornton Reservoir

✉ Reservoir Road, Thornton, Leicestershire

☎ 01332 865081

🖳 www.stwater.co.uk

Thornton Reservoir nestles below the village of Thornton and is a popular spot for walkers. This waterside path is a fantastic ORPing trail that circumnavigates the reservoir with extensive views across the water to the wonderful rolling Leicestershire countryside. There are plenty of picnic spots along the way – an easy stroll for the whole family.

Location: Thornton Water, OS Map 140, GR 471074

Distance: Circular, 5km

Terrain: Flat, broad, loose stone track

Facilities: Car park; toilets; visitor centre incorporating exhibition room and fishing lodge; sculpture trail. Coffee shop across the road at Thornton Nurseries, and there are two pubs in the village.

The Route

1. Set off from the main car park, under the canopy of large Douglas fir trees. The first point of interest you will come across is the visitor centre; this is a good viewpoint too.

2. Rounding the left horn of the reservoir provides fantastic views across the water and to the surrounding countryside. Take a bench and enjoy them – we did!

3. Keep on ORPing and to the left of the track you will see a footpath leading into the woods. The footpath follows a crescent-shaped route back to the main path.

   This is the East Midland Shape Sculpture Trail, and the route takes you through some lovely woodland to "The Bird Totems". These

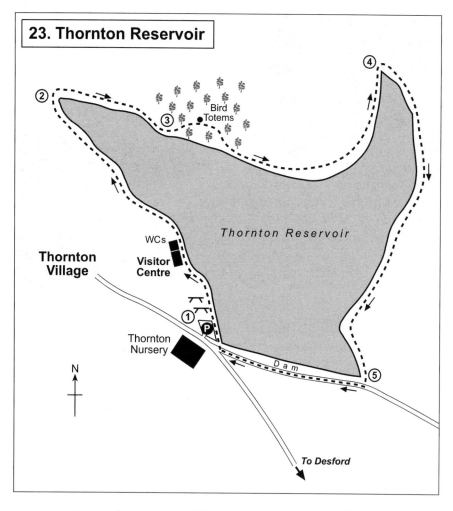

23. Thornton Reservoir

interesting sculptures carved from tree stumps are definitely worth the detour.

4. Follow the lakeshore around the right-hand horn of the reservoir and continue along this lakeshore path to the road.

5. At the road, turn right and follow the pavement along the wall of the dam, back to the car park.

The view along the left horn of the reservoir

Tropical Birdland

✉ Linbridge Lane, Desford, Leicestershire, LE9 9GN

☎ 01455 824603

You could combine your trip to Thornton with a trip to Tropical Birdland. Wander the acres of woodland with aviaries brimming with colourful, singing birds. Watch out though as many of the birds are free to fly and if they take a liking to you, may perch on your shoulder!

24. Vicar Water

✉ New Clipstone, Nottinghamshire

☎ 01623 466340

🖥 www.greenwoodforest.org.uk

On the western fringe of Sherwood Forest nestles the award winning Vicar Water, a great find for ORPers with its excellent network of paths, and dramatic views. The parkland is based on reclaimed spoil tips associated with the nearby Clipstone Colliery that has the tallest winding gear in the country. The tracks run around and over the hill and are not to be missed, due to the excellent views over Sherwood Pines, Clipstone and the surrounding hills.

Location: OS Map 120 GR 588627

Distance: Circular, 3km

Terrain: Gravel and loose stone tracks, one ascent. This route is unsuitable for double buggies and less-sturdy four-wheelers.

Facilities: Car park; toilets; visitor centre incorporating refreshments and information

The Route

1. From the car park ignore the stile to the lake area, but bear right along the crushed stone path that runs parallel to the lakes.

2. Follow the track as it passes farmland – one of Toby's favourite baa-ing spots, as sheep graze close to the path in the adjacent field. The track will soon bear right over a bridge, and continue ahead before reaching a stile (where you can pass to the side). Bear left on the bridleway with arable land to the right.

3. Pass through the first iron-gate to the left of the track. This will lead to another gate adjacent to a Vicar Water information board. Pass through this gate and continue up the hill on a broad loose

24. Vicar Water

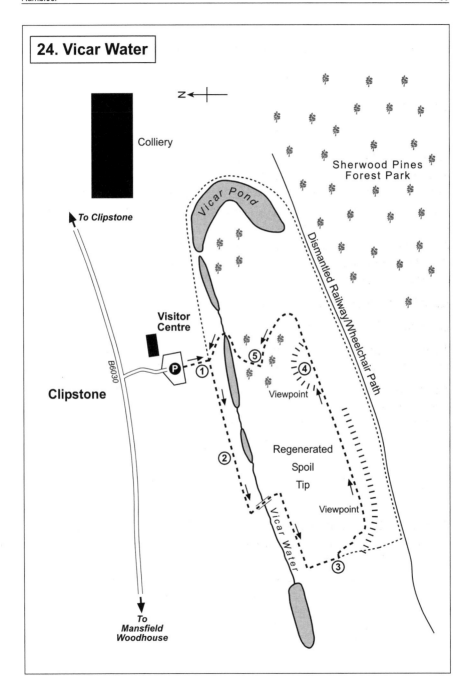

Summit view – the former Clipstone Colliery's winding gear is said to be the highest in the country.

stone track. This is an easy climb to the summit. At the top of the hill is an excellently placed bench that commands great views over Clipstone and the Colliery.

4. From the bench continue on the same path towards the gate. After the gate continue straight ahead. (Do not be tempted to turn right down to Vicar Pond, as this track has a steep descent ending in a high stile – and believe me, it is a steep ascent back up).

5. When the lake opposite the car park comes into view, take the right turn off the path, and return to the car park.

Note: There is an alternative wheelchair path that leads you around the base of the hill, and over to Vicar Pond. It is totally flat along an excellent compact track. It is definitely worth a push if you have a double buggy or less sturdy four-wheeler, or if you simply fancy an Amble instead.

25. Watermead Country Park

✉ Syston near Leicester

☎ 0116 267 1944

🖥 www.leics.gov.uk

Watermead is a wildlife wonderland hosting a collection of lakes and ponds, a nature reserve and woodland, together with the River Soar and the Grand Union Canal. If that's not enough there are impressive weirs, a life-size woolly mammoth, and entertaining water sports to see all just 5 miles north of Leicester city centre.

Location: OS Map 140, GR 604086

Distance: Circular, 6km

Terrain: Surfaced tracks, with a short grass section

Facilities: Car park; toilets on site; Brewsters family restaurant at entrance to South car park; and The Mulberry Tree public house located en route.

The Route

1. From the southerly based Alderton Close car park , bear left passing under the woolly mammoth sculpture and continue round the track passing the weir, to the lock. Cross two bridges, and bear right along the riverside path passing The Mulberry Tree, excellent for a bite to eat. The path re-enters the Park after approximately 300 metres via a large kissing gate.

2. Follow signs to Meadow Lane car park. When you pass the car park to the left, continue straight ahead following signs to King Lear's Lake. Look out for the rabbits.

3. As track bears right you will see a large arched bridge crossing to King Lear's Lake. Cross the bridge and bear left passing the sculpture in the water. There are well-located picnic tables around the lake, but beware of the swans as they are used to being fed.

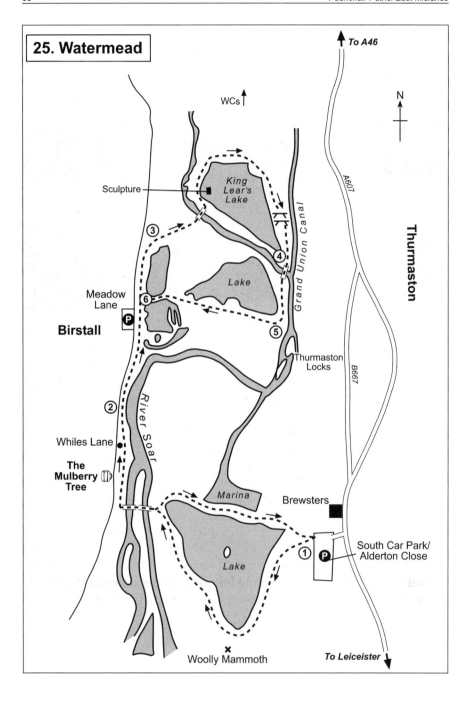

25. Watermead

To A46

N

WCs

Sculpture

King Lear's Lake

Grand Union Canal

Thurmaston

A607

③

④

Lake

Meadow Lane

⑥

Birstall

P

⑤

Thurmaston Locks

B667

②

River Soar

Whiles Lane

The Mulberry Tree

Marina

Brewsters

Lake

① P

South Car Park/ Alderton Close

Woolly Mammoth

To Leiceister

Boardwalks and weirs at Watermead

4. After almost circumnavigating the lake pass through the first kissing gate you see to the left of the track, and cross the bridge and subsequent boardwalk on top of the weir. Continue straight ahead along the grass bordering the Grand Union Canal.

5. When you reach the fork in the canal follow the sign to "Thurmaston Mill Lane" keeping the Nature Reserve to your right. Before reaching the Lane, you will approach Thurmaston Locks. Here, bear right following signs to "Meadow Lane car park" along a surfaced path flanked by lakes and reed beds.

6. At Meadow Lane car park bear left following signs to "Whiles Lane". Retrace your steps on the path by the River Soar passing The Mulberry Tree, and cross the two bridges back into the park. Return to the car park bearing left around the lake via the boardwalk, with an excellent view of the woolly mammoth.

26. Wollaton Park

✉ Wollaton Hall and Park, Wollaton, Nottingham, NG8 2AE

☎ 0115 9153900

🖳 www.wollatonhall.org.uk

This deer park has a wonderful mixture of things to see and do, from an Industrial Museum to a Natural History Museum, and a large lakeland area to a secluded woodland, all only a few miles from Nottingham city centre. The ORP route passes through prime deer spotting sites, skirts the perimeter of the Hall, and follows the lakeside. ORPing in the Park is top notch for buggy or 3-wheeler!

Location: OS Map 129, GR 529398

Distance: Circular, 3km

Terrain: Surfaced paths

Facilities: Car park; toilets; baby changing located in the Hall; coffee shop; Industrial Museum; Steam Engine House; Natural History Museum; gift shop; Yard Gallery; children's play area.

The Route

1. From the main car park take the tree-lined tarmac path towards Wollaton Hall. There is a slight ascent on this path but nothing too taxing.

2. Follow signs to the Industrial Museum. Walk through the yard passing the Museum to your right. Pass under two archways before you reach a fine view of the parkland and lake below. From this vantage point you will see an iron door located within the wall of the formal gardens, (to the left of the last bench perched on the hilltop ahead). Pass through the door and follow the cobbled path up to the formal gardens of the Hall.

3. Bear to the right around the gardens, and pass through the gate over the dry moat. Follow the mature tree-lined path down to the

"Toddle-tastic" paths around Wollaton Hall, a grand Tudor building completed in 1588.

lake. This is "toddle-tastic" country as the parkland provides a great place to let the little ones out to stretch their legs.

4. At the large reedbed follow the track to the left towards Thompson's Wood, a large broad-leaved woodland area. The path is wide but quite secluded as the trees tower above, and large rhododendron bushes line the path. Coming out of the woods you will see a disused boathouse. From the boathouse, the views up to Wollaton Hall are stunning.

Keep an ear free for the calls of different birds and you'll be surprised by how many you can hear in all seasons.

5. When you reach the northern shore of the lake, you may notice that this is a prime duck feeding area. It is also a grand spot to take a break and watch the huge variety of resident and migratory wildfowl.

If you are lucky you may catch the deer taking a splash over to the island in the lake – quite a spectacle, and a noisy one at that as the deer invade the private space of the ducks!

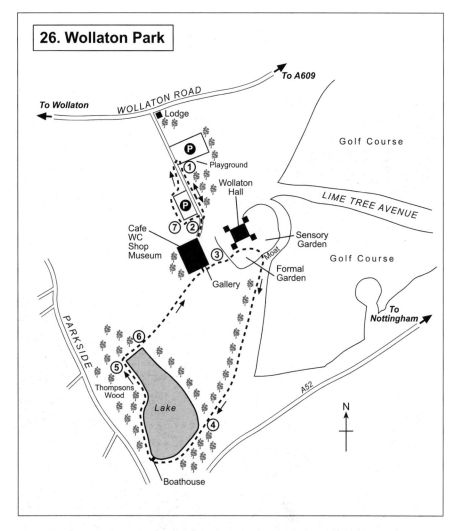

26. Wollaton Park

6. Looking up towards the Hall cross the bridge, and walk up towards the clock tower and archway again. Retrace your steps under the arch and through the cobbled yard.

7. At the upper car park follow the left-hand path back to the main car park. The grassland to the left is a favourite spot for deer, so keep your eyes peeled.

Epics!

Epic pushchair paths at Bradgate Park (Walk 28)

27. Birklands and Budby

☒ Sherwood Forest Country Park, Edwinstowe, Mansfield,
Nottinghamshire NG21 9HN

☎ 01623 823202

💻 www.nottinghamshire.gov.uk

*If getting away from the crowds is what you long for, then this Epic
should fit the bill. Beginning in Edwinstowe, the route leads you
under the canopy of ancient trees, out to open heathland, before
returning you to Edwinstowe via the Major Oak. We felt like we
were in the depths of the Scottish countryside on this route as there
were few people around and hardly any civilisation in sight – quite a
feat in the Midlands.*

Location: Sherwood Forest Country Park, OS Map 120 GR625673

Distance: Circular, 7km

Terrain: Undulating, woodland trails and sandy heathland paths

Facilities: Car park; toilets and refreshments at the Craft Centre
opposite the car park. Or you could pop down the road to the
Watermill Tea Shop in Ollerton and experience award winning tea and
homemade cakes (Winner of the Tea Council Award for 2005).

The Route

1. From Edwinstowe car park, bear left through the fairground site
   towards the woods. Follow the path into the woods signed
   "Bridleway to Gleadthorpe". Look out for the twisted tree sculptures along the route. The path soon descends to a junction.

2. Take the first left passing a metal gate, and continue along the
   Robin Hood Way until you reach Centre Tree. This is an excellent
   broad woodland track. You will know when you've reached
   Centre Tree as there is a large firebreak in the forest, where the
   National Cycle Route bisects the track.

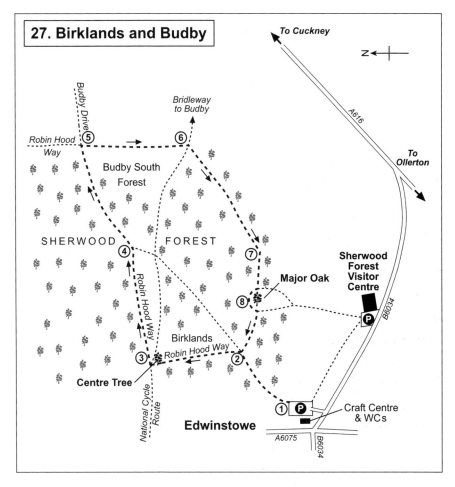

27. Birklands and Budby

To Cuckney

To Ollerton

Bridleway to Budby

Budby Drive

Robin Hood Way ⑤ → ⑥

Budby South Forest

SHERWOOD ④ FOREST ⑦

Sherwood Forest Visitor Centre

Major Oak

Robin Hood Way

⑧

Birklands

Robin Hood Way ③ ②

Centre Tree

National Cycle Route

Edwinstowe

① Ⓟ

Craft Centre & WCs

A6075

B6034

B6034

A616

3. At Centre Tree bear immediately right and continue through attractive silver birch woodland – beware of cyclists as this is a cycle route too.

4. At the next junction, ignore the trails to the Major Oak; instead continue ahead on the bridleway to Budby South Forest. The landscape changes to heathland, mixed with pockets of pine and silver birch woodland. This is where we get that distinctly Scottish feeling – although thankfully we haven't had the weather to match! There is a conservation grazing area to the right.

Tree sculpture in Sherwood Forest

5. When you reach the next junction bear right following signs to "Budby". There is arable land to the left and the Dukeries Army Training Area to the right.

6. After a short incline, you will approach two tracks leading into heathland on the right of the path. Take the second bridleway passing through a large gate. Follow the bridleway straight crossing the forestry track and continuing to the busier Major Oak path.

7. Bear right following signs to the "Major Oak".

8. You will know when you've reached the Major Oak as it is the big tree surrounded by a fence with its lower branches assisted by scaffolding – an awesome sight nonetheless. At the Oak follow the sign to "Edwinstowe Village". After 200m there are several paths criss-crossing the track so simply follow the sign to "Fairground", and this will lead you back to Edwinstowe car park. In the summer there is a fairground located by Edwinstowe car park.

28. Bradgate Hilltops

✉ Bradgate Park Trust, Estate Office, Deer Barn Buildings, Bradgate Park, Newtown Linford, Leicester, LE6 0HE

☎ 0116 236 2713

A walk with maximum return in summer or winter. This route takes you through some of the best safe off-road tracks that the East Midlands has to offer. There are rocky outcrops, large woodlands, the folly of Old John Tower, ditches to cross, and rutted tracks to contend with. This Epic is demanding. We have completed this route with a flat tyre (it was so muddy we didn't notice!) in the depths of winter and it was excellent fun – whatever takes your fancy.

Location: OS Map 129 GR 523116

Distance: Circular, 4.5km

Terrain: Grass tracks with steep ascents and descents. Recommended for all-terrain pushchairs only.

Facilities: Car park; toilets; tea rooms and gift shop at Newtown Linford car park; numerous picnic areas.

The Route

1. From Hunts Hill car park follow the broad grass track up to the Monolith to the right of Old John Tower. This is a World War 1 Memorial, and presents excellent views over the parkland. It is a gentle climb at first, but then becomes steep and rocky towards the top.

2. Looking towards Old John Tower you will see a dry stone wall circling a woodland area. Pass through the gateway in the wall into the sheltered woodland area, good for a picnic on a blustery day. Following the loose stone path across the woodland pass through the gateway on the opposite wall. There is one step up, then follow the track to the left of the tower, and on up to the top.

This is fairly steep ORPing but great fun, and the views are well worth the effort. There is a toposcope on the summit.

3. Looking down the hill in an easterly direction follow the broad grass track towards the large rock outcrop on the hillock below. You will pass by smaller crags on the descent before you ascend to the outcrop.

Tough pushchair terrain at Bradgate – passing by the large rock outcrop in the foreground

4. Directly behind the rock outcrop is a fenced off plantation which you should keep to your left as you reach the brow of the hill. With a new vantage point, follow the broad grass path in an easterly direction down the hill towards two fenced-off plantations, crossing two shallow ditches on the way. Walk between the plantations, and drop down to the surfaced path by Cropston reservoir.

5. Bear left towards Hallgates car park. (Alternatively, if you fancy some refreshments you can bear right and follow the path to Newtown Linford car park, and then retrace your steps back to Hallgates and continue the Loop. See Walk 2.)

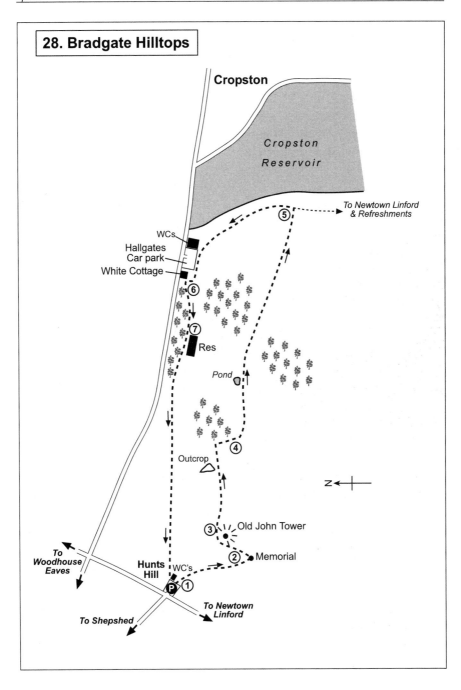

28. Bradgate Hilltops

Cropston

Cropston Reservoir

To Newtown Linford & Refreshments

WCs

Hallgates Car park

White Cottage

Res

Pond

Outcrop

Old John Tower

Memorial

To Woodhouse Eaves

Hunts Hill

WC's

To Newtown Linford

To Shepshed

6. Before you enter the car park, bear left and follow the grass track beside the dry stone wall. The track soon bears right passing a quaint white cottage, and then continues running parallel to the wall beside woodland.

7. Pass to the right of the covered reservoir and continue straight. This is a fairly steep push, but you are rewarded with excellent views of the route you have completed.

Finish this route at Hunts Hill car park.

29. Hemlock Stone

✉ Bramcote Hills Open Space, Broxtowe, Nottingham

🖥 www.broxtowe.gov.uk

Bramcote Hills and the Hemlock Stone are located to the south west of Nottingham and provide a great location for an ORPing day out. This is a wonderful route that is both steep and demanding, leading you round prime mountain biking terrain. You begin in the gentle woodland of Bramcote Hills, then it's across to the ancient Hemlock Stone, and over to Stapleford Park for a great picnic site and a well deserved rest! This one will get your heart racing and its well worth the effort just for that feeling of accomplishment at the end of the day!

Location: OS Map 129 GR 500385

Distance: Circular round Bramcote Hills, and there and back to Stapleford Park, 3.2km

Terrain: Undulating, loose stone track, may be muddy when wet. This route contains broad steps.

Facilities: Car park; picnic area; children's play area; trim trail.

Note: If you don't fancy an Epic, Bramcote Hills parkland is a prime "toddle-tastic" area, ideal for a picnic – and there is often an ice cream van parked in the summer.

The Route

1. From the car park, you can see the children's play area. Behind the playground is an excellent surfaced path, which will lead you along the foot of the woodlands. You will pass the site of Bramcote Hills House and some excellent picnic areas.

2. After approximately 500m, follow the sign to "Bramcote Hills" which bears left into the woodland. The track leads you up some broad steps and then bears left contouring around the hill on an undulating path. There are excellent views over Nottingham.

Please ignore all the mountain bike tracks up to the summit area to the left of the track. We tried the summit push for research reasons (and not because Antony likes to walk to the top of everything in sight) and trust us, you need crampons and a disc brake to return in one piece! Toby loved it but the pram brake was steaming and it was our old knees that took the brunt of the descent – we do not recommend it.

3. The path descends via broad steps to the children's play area again. Bear right and follow signs to the walled gardens for a well-deserved rest. Across the thoroughfare, you will see the amazing Hemlock Stone balanced on the hillside opposite.

4. Cross the road at the traffic lights, turn right and enter the wilds of Stapleford Park. Head up the path bearing to the right to reach the Hemlock Stone.

5. With the Stone behind you, ignore the tracks leading up the hill as these are steep; instead follow the path that bears left around

The weather sculptured Hemlock Stone

29. The Hemlock Stone

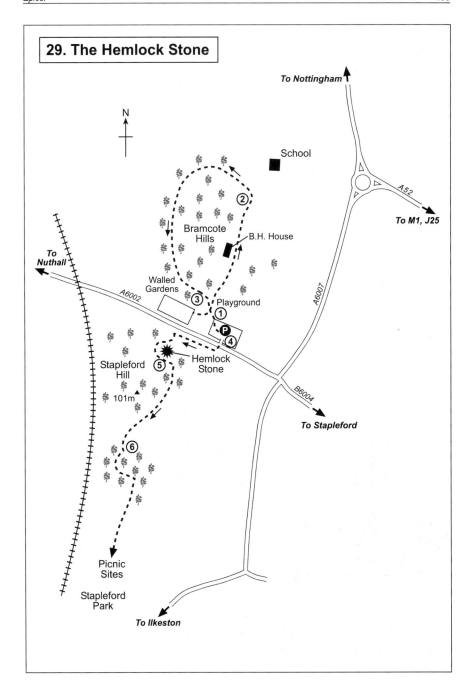

the hill. This path will lead you behind the houses to a broad descent into farmland.

6. Cross to the side of the small bridge – there is no water but it may be muddy – and bear immediately left into woodland along a narrow track, which soon opens out to a broad gravel track. After another 150 metres when the path forks bear right over the hillside and you will find yourself in wonderful open parkland. This is a lovely place to rest and enjoy a picnic before retracing your steps back to Bramcote Hills car park.

30. Linacre Reservoirs

✉ Cutthorpe, Derbyshire

☎ 01246 551035

The Linacre reservoirs are set in an attractive wooded valley north west of Chesterfield. The site is owned by Severn Trent Water and consists of three small reservoirs, one flowing into the next by an interesting network of weirs and water steps. This route contours around the steep valley sides passing the lower and middle waters, to the upper reservoir. The tracks are good but there are a couple of steep sections that certainly require good footwear so this has been categorised as Epic – don't forget your picnic, and enjoy the views.

Location: OS Map 119 GR 337726, entrance via Cutthorpe B6050

Distance: Circular, 3km

Terrain: Woodland tracks. Good footwear recommended.

Facilities: Car park (continue driving until you reach the "No vehicles beyond this point" sign and park); toilets; baby changing; picnic sites; The Peacock Inn along the Cutthorpe road provides good food.

For an easier route – if you wish to visit Linacre without undertaking an Epic route, you still can! Simply take the road down from the car park as in point (1) and pass through the first kissing gate to the right, before you reach the Rangers Office. You can then follow the track along the northern shores of the lower and middle reservoirs and return the same way. This would be categorised as a Ramble – so get going and feast your eyes upon this interesting valley.

The Route

1. From the lower car park bear left down the road until you reach the Rangers office and toilets. From here you can either push down the steps, or take the track to the left of the steps down to the dam of the lower reservoir. The track is steep and may be slip-

30. Linacre Reservoirs

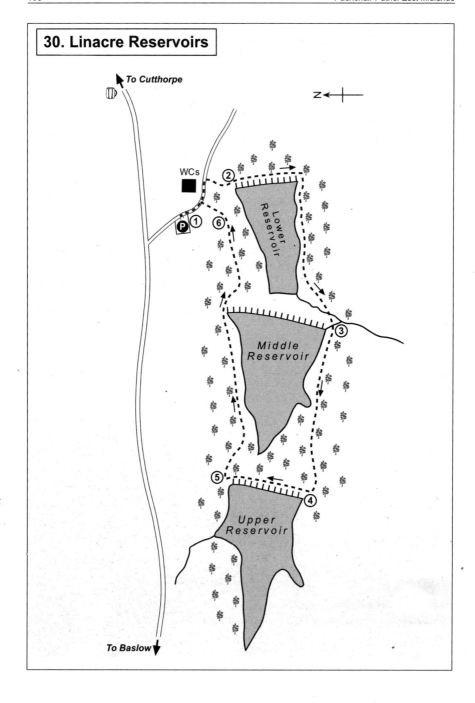

pery when muddy so take extra care. We needed to use the disc brake on our pram for the lower section of the track.

2. Cross the lower reservoir dam wall, and bear immediately right along the shore path through woodland. This is a lovely stretch of track that weaves between the trees before a short but steep descent followed by a short ascent up to the middle reservoir dam.

3. Continue straight ahead along the southern shores of the middle reservoir. You may encounter cheeky squirrels darting around the fir and pine trees along the way.

4. When you reach the upper reservoir you will see an impressive weir that precedes a succession of water steps that transports the water down to the middle reservoir. Cross the dam – this provides

The view from the upper reservoir, down to the middle reservoir.

an excellent vantage point across the upper reservoir and sweeping views through the trees to the middle reservoir and beyond.

Note: If you wish to continue around the upper reservoir you will
reach wooden bridges preceded by narrow steps, on each shore,
in addition to a boardwalk for part of the way round the southern
shore. We do not recommend circumnavigating the upper reservoir with a pushchair.

5. Bear right along the northern shore of the middle reservoir. This
   broad track contours above the reservoir and is a lovely woodland
   walk. Continue past the dam of the middle reservoir and follow
   the track by the lower reservoir up to the gate.

6. Pass through the kissing gate and bear left up the road back to the
   car park.

   When the reservoirs were first established it is said that the rich used
   the water to water their gardens, the middle classes used it to wash
   their clothes and the poor used it to make soup! Who knows who uses
   it these days!